ISRAEL

Jack Altman

J·P·M
PUBLICATIONS

CONTENTS

This Way Israel	**3**
Flashback	**7**
Three Faiths	**15**
On the Scene	**19**
Jerusalem	*19*
Old City 19, Outside the Walls 24, Modern City Centre 25, Eastern Jerusalem 27, Western Outskirts 28, Excursions 29	
Wilderness and Desert	*31*
Judaean Wilderness 31, Dead Sea 32, The Negev 34	
Galilee	*36*
Tiberias 36, Sea of Galilee 37, Safed 39, Nazareth 41	
Tel Aviv and the Mediterranean	*43*
Tel Aviv 43, Jaffa 46, Caesarea 48, Haifa 48, Acre 50	
Red Sea	*53*
Eilat 53, Timna 53	
Shopping	**55**
Dining Out	**57**
Sports	**59**
The Hard Facts	**60**
Index	*64*

Fold out maps

Israel, Around Jerusalem, Central Jerusalem, Old City, Tel Aviv, Haifa

This Way Israel

The Formidable Shock

People are never blasé when they go to Israel. To say that this little bit of territory arouses strong feelings in atheist, Christian, Jew or Muslim alike (the precedence here is purely alphabetical) is to state the obvious. But no warning quite prepares you for the jolt, emotional and even physical, of your actual encounter with this holy, unholy land.

Rising from the golden Judaean hills, the ancient city of Jerusalem provokes emotions that are deep, disturbing and exhilarating—wonder, awe, anger, joy, but never indifference. The temple of Solomon, the Passion of Jesus, the miraculous journey of the Prophet Mohammed have all left their mark. On the coast, in emphatically secular contrast, the bright, cocky, modern metropolis of Tel Aviv delights newcomers with its cosmopolitan cafés, dynamic art galleries and theatres. Chronically impatient Tel-Avivians have long settled for a largely uninviting architecture, and they are only now taking the time to give their city the graceful style it deserves. That, too, comes as a surprise.

Land of milk and honey it was, and is again. The familiar 20th-century image of Israel being a "nation carved out of the desert" has lost none of its dramatic impact. Orchards, vineyards, olive groves, and new forests of pine and eucalyptus spread from Galilee, the Valley of Jezreel and the fertile coastal plain ever further down to the Judaean Wilderness and the great triangle of the Negev desert that covers more than half of Israel's total land surface.

And the people? With all the wars they have gone through, they would have reason enough to be a bunch of nervous wrecks, jumping at every car that backfires. Not at all. From time to time, fanatics and extremists grab the headlines, but for the vast majority life goes on. Young and old, they remain astonishingly cheerful and easy-going. Take a leaf out of the Israelis' book, it's a good one.

Promised Land

Throughout history, Israel's destiny has been that of a much-trampled corridor between Egypt and Africa to the west and Asia and Arabia to the east and south. Only 150 km (93 miles) across at its widest point, the skimpy strip of land hugging the Mediterranean measures just 450 km (280 miles) from its northern border with Lebanon down to Eilat on the Gulf of Aqaba and Egypt's Sinai peninsula. To the east are Syria and Jordan.

The densely populated coastal plain contains more than two-thirds of the country's 5 million inhabitants. In the north, Haifa is Israel's main port and third largest city. This industrial and commercial centre boasts two important universities, notably the Technion for engineers. Across the bay, old Acre has kept intact its Crusader citadel and handsome buildings of the Ottoman era. South of Haifa, orchards, olive groves and vineyards hug the slopes of Mount Carmel. Down the coast, the ancient Roman port of Caesarea hosts an annual summer music festival in its amphitheatre. In addition to the cultural and business activities, Tel Aviv has its share of beach hotels, with neighbouring Jaffa adding a colourful ancient touch as the port from which Jonah sailed to his close encounter with a big fish.

The green hills of Galilee form the geographical backbone of the country. The tallest peak is Mount Meron, 1,208 m (3,963 ft). It has long been fertile in both agriculture and spiritual fervour. Christian pilgrims flock to Nazareth as the home of Jesus, to nearby Mount Tabor, scene of his Transfiguration, and the Sea of Galilee where he and his fishermen spread their word. For Jews, the modern lake resort of Tiberias began as a seat of Talmudic scholarship after the Romans' Destruction of the Second Temple. In the northern hills, Safed has been a centre of Kabbalists and other mystics since the Jews were expelled from Catholic Spain in 1492—joined today by a motley crew of markedly less inspired artists. With fresh water fast becoming a more important issue than oil in Middle East politics, the lake itself is a major focus of Israel's sensitive relations with Syria and Jordan. A canal built in the 1960s siphons off the lake's water from the Jordan River to serve Israel's coastal region and all the way south to the Negev Desert.

South of Galilee, the more arid hills of Samaria and Judaea, which since 1967 formed Israel's Occupied Territories, are gradually reverting to Palestinian administration. Among the most interesting places of this region are Jericho, the world's most ancient city, Jesus' birthplace in Bethlehem and, when tempers settle, the Muslim and Jewish shrines associated with Abraham in Hebron.

The strictly Israeli part of the Judaean Hills embracing Jerusalem rolls down in a splendid wilderness to the Dead Sea. Sparse pastures are grazed by flocks of goats and sheep. Their Bedouin herdsmen still occupy caves that once provided refuge for the prophet Elijah and for the Essenes' Dead Sea Scrolls at Qumran. Dead Sea resorts offer soothing mud baths after the obligatory unsinkable salt dip, in addition to Ein Gedi's magnificent nature reserve. At the southern end of the sea is the historic fortress of Masada, heroically, tragically defended by Jewish rebels and zealots against the Romans in AD 73.

The great Rift Valley, beginning in Turkey and thrusting through the Dead Sea deep into Africa, ends its Israeli section at Eilat. King Solomon's port attracts today's sun-lizards to its beaches. Divers come for the beautiful coral and rich marine life of the gulf that forms an arm of the Red Sea.

The Pot's Not for Melting

For sheer ethnic diversity, New York has nothing on Israel. Quite apart from the Arabs—Muslim and Christian—the Jews come not only from Poland, Russia and other ex-Soviet Republics, but also from every country in Europe, North Africa, the Gulf states, the Far East, North and South America. And you will soon discover that "looking Jewish" does not mean much any more. Over the centuries, there has been enough intermarriage for Israelis to look like everybody under the sun.

In the past, the distinction between Ashkenazi Jews from Central and Eastern Europe and Sephardic Jews scattered by the Spanish expulsion through North Africa and the Balkans caused political and social conflicts. Today, the differences in temperament, in cultural traditions, cuisine and forms of worship endure. The prejudices will vanish only with peace and prosperity.

POPULATION AND PRICKLY PEARS

Israel's total population is estimated at 5,900,000, of which about four-fifths (4,702,000) are Jews. Israeli Arab Muslims number around 868,000, Christians (mostly Arab) 126,000. The rest, numbering some 97,000, are in the main Druze (an ancient breakaway sect from Islam). Of the Jewish population, 64 per cent are native-born Israelis, known as sabras, a nickname that in Hebrew also means the indigenous prickly pear. The others, born outside Israel, are 20 per cent European, North and South American, and 16 per cent African and Asian.

Flashback

Beginnings

As modern headlines testify, the histories of Israel and Palestine are inextricably linked. The region's earliest known remains of human beings, dating back to 600,000 BC, were found in the Jordan Valley; they were active as hunters of large animals in what is now both Israeli and Palestinian territory.

In this early Stone Age, they used flint tools and mastered the use of fire around 200,000 BC. Grain farming and cattle herding emerged in 14,000 BC. Founded around 8300 BC, Jericho can claim to be the world's oldest continuously inhabited town.

By the time copper and bronze came into use (3000 BC), the largely arid region known as Canaan was divided into modest city-states, while the fertile Nile and Euphrates river valleys were producing the great empires of Egypt and Mesopotamia.

From Abraham to Moses

Archaeologists see in the Bible a useful guide to actual events in

In the Garden of Gethsemane, golden onion domes above the Basilica of the Agony.

Israel's story. Mesopotamian cattle-herders like Abraham did indeed cross the Jordan river (1800 BC) to seek out the greener pastures of Egypt before deciding to stay in Canaan. Semitic clans like Jacob's were driven by famine to settle in the Nile Delta.

Outside the Bible, scholars have no documentary evidence of Moses. They accept, however, that Hebrew peasants in the Nile Delta were employed in seasonal forced labour on monumental construction sites, as suggested in Exodus 1, 11. A charismatic leader like Moses could well have led the oppressed Hebrews across the Sinai and into their Promised Land. The monotheistic ideas he propagated from Mount Sinai may be a powerful refinement of those of the maverick pharaoh, Akhenaton.

Israelites and Philistines

If Joshua did lead the Hebrew exiles across the Jordan river to Jericho (1200 BC), their conquest of Canaan took much longer than the triumphant Biblical account. Israel is the Biblical name accorded first to Jacob, then to the new nation of his sons' tribes (its meaning is disputed, perhaps "God rules"). Their loose confed-

FLASHBACK

eration extended from Dan in the north—now a nature reserve near the Golan Heights—down to Beersheba in the Negev desert.

Meanwhile, new non-Semitic settlers, whom the Israelites called Philistines, had appeared on the coast. Perhaps originating from Crete, they brought iron weapons and technology and left their name on the land of Palestine. Their tight political control of the coastal plain prompted the hill-dwelling Israelites to close ranks in a unified kingdom under Saul in 1025 BC, but his troubled reign ended in defeat and suicide.

David and Solomon
For Saul's successor, the people turned to the heroic slayer of Goliath. Musician, poet and man of passion, King David seized Jerusalem from the Jebusites in 1005 BC and made it his capital. David affirmed his spiritual leadership by setting the Ark of the Covenant on the rock where the first Temple was to be erected. The Temple was built on a grandiose scale by his son Solomon (c. 965–928 BC); it was as much the symbol of his flourishing commercial empire as of the Israelites' god it was intended to glorify. But the people objected to the heavy taxes that Solomon imposed, and to the favouritism he showed towards his tribe of Judah.

Israel in Turmoil
Following Solomon's death, two kingdoms emerged: Judah, with Jerusalem as its capital, in the south; and Israel in the north, with its capital at Samaria near Shechem (modern Nablus). The

---

1

THE BEST ARCHEOLOGICAL SITE Israeli scholars have done a remarkable job in the past 30 years in excavating and restoring ancient Canaanite, Israelite, Greek, Roman, Byzantine and Crusader monuments. Without fanciful and deceptive "renovation", they have made sites easily accessible and well explained for laymen (in English and Hebrew). One of the most spectacular is **Bet She'an** in the Jordan Valley south of the Sea of Galilee. Among 18 levels of settlement uncovered from the Stone Age to the Arab invasion are remains of Egyptian temples and palaces and a magnificent Roman theatre.

Jewish nation was ravaged by internal strife, assassinations and palace revolutions; while the prophets railed against tyranny and idolatry.

In the 8th century BC, the Assyrians invaded from the east. In 722, they deported Samaritans as slaves, replacing them with colonists from Mesopotamia. A few hundred descendants of the tiny remnant still dwell on the outskirts of Nablus. In the south, only Jerusalem held out, spurred on by the prophet Isaiah. The Assyrians retreated but remained in control of both kingdoms.

A century later, Babylon ended Assyrian supremacy. The Egyptians briefly filled the vacuum in Palestine but were driven out around 605 by Babylon's King Nebuchadnezzar. The prophet Jeremiah, who castigated social injustice and immorality as the cause of the Jews' disintegration, advised against suicidal resistance. Jerusalem finally fell in 587, its Temple destroyed and its inhabitants carried off to captivity.

Exile and Return

The 50 years of exile in Babylon were less arduous than the serfdom in Egypt. The Israelites learned new skills in farming, weaving, dyeing, metalwork and banking. In 538, Babylon's new master, Persian emperor Cyrus, let the Jews return to their homeland. Some 40,000 settled a reduced province, known henceforth as Judaea, and went on to rebuild the Temple.

Following the conquest of the Persians in 332 by Alexander the Great, his Greek successors in Egypt, the Ptolemies, annexed the land they called Palestine and appointed a high priest in Jerusalem to govern the province of Judaea.

By the year 200, control passed to the Ptolemies' Greek rivals, the Seleucids. In 169, they seized Jerusalem and converted the Temple to the cult of Zeus. Two years later, the Hasmonean family—better known as the Maccabees or "hammers"—led a heroic revolt. Their spectacular guerrilla warfare against the Greeks culminated in recapture and purification of the Temple. Beset by Babylonians in the east and Romans in the west, the Greeks left the Maccabees in control of Judaea, extending their rule to Samaria in 128.

Herod and Jesus

Herod became undisputed ruler of Judaea by 37 BC. Ironically, the man known as King of the Jews and builder of the Second Temple was despised by the Jews themselves as a despot. In fact he was Jewish only by conversion imposed by the Maccabees.

Flashback

Monastery of St George, near old Jericho, in a daunting biblical setting.

It was perhaps two years before Herod's death in 4 BC that Jesus was born in Bethlehem. There is evidence to confirm that he grew up in Nazareth and was preaching in Galilee around AD 27. Pontius Pilate, Roman governor in Palestine (AD 26–36), had Jesus executed apparently for the perceived threat that the Christian movement posed to Roman law and order.

Revolt and Second Exile

In the year 70, four years after a first Jewish revolt had been crushed, Jerusalem was taken and the Temple destroyed by Titus, the Roman commander. Today, only the Western Wall remains. On the Dead Sea, Jewish zealots' last resistance at Masada ended in the communal suicide of 960 men, women and children. Roman historian Tacitus set the number of deaths in the revolt at 600,000 (the Jewish population at the time is estimated at 4 million). Thousands more were sold into slavery and deported to Rome, starting the Diaspora to western Europe.

In 132, Emperor Hadrian drove all remaining Jews out of Jerusalem. As their empire declined, the Romans left the people of Palestine in a welcome state of benign neglect.

Byzantine Era
Three centuries after the Crucifixion, Helena, the mother of Emperor Constantine, visited Palestine to identify the sites associated with the life of Jesus. In around 326, she found pieces of the True Cross in Jerusalem and the stable of Jesus' birth in Bethlehem. Churches and shrines were subsequently built over the sites, attracting pilgrims from all over Europe. Jews were once more banished from Jerusalem, principally to farm villages in Galilee, the Jezreel Valley and the Negev.

In 614, the Persians seized Jerusalem and carried off many of its inhabitants and the True Cross. King Chosroes closed the churches and gave the city to the Jews, but he took it back again three years later. The Byzantines counterattacked, and by 629 the Christians and the True Cross were back in place—until the arrival of the Arabs.

Islam in Palestine
Though Mohammed's visit to Jerusalem has not been historically documented, Islam bases its attachment to the city on a belief in his night-time journey from the Temple Mount to heaven. In 638, six years after the Prophet's death, the Arabs seized Jerusalem in their conquest of Palestine. In 691, the Dome of the Rock was built over the spot from which Mohammed made his heavenly journey.

For 300 years, Jews and Christians were treated with great respect until caught in the crossfire of Sunni and Shi'ite factions. El-Hakim (996–1021), of the Shi'ite Fatimid dynasty, persecuted Sunni Muslims, Jews and Christians alike. In 1009, he destroyed the Holy Sepulchre and other Christian shrines, proclaiming himself the earthly incarnation of Allah. His return is awaited by the Druze sect, present today in Galilee, the Golan and Lebanon.

The Crusaders
In 1071, Sunni Muslim Turks drove the Shi'ite Fatimids out of Jerusalem and closed the holy places to Christian pilgrims. This and the general Islamic assault on the Byzantine Empire prompted Pope Urban II to launch the First Crusade. In 1099, two armies invaded Palestine from the north. On entering Jerusalem, the Crusaders first killed the Jews hiding in the synagogue before turning on the Muslims the Pope had sent them to deal with. Over the next 20 years, divisions in Muslim forces enabled the Crusaders to continue their indiscriminate massacre of Jews and Arabs and thus to consolidate their Kingdom of Jerusalem. These champions of Christian civilization installed

Flashback

Street lads preside over sales of a variety of fresh bread—even bagels.

a highly efficient feudal administration, built a new Holy Sepulchre and a magnificent series of churches and castles throughout the land.

By the 1160s, the Muslims had turned the tide with victories over the Crusaders in Syria and Egypt. Saladin, Sultan of Egypt, smashed the Frankish armies and captured Jerusalem in 1187, bestowing its present Arab name, *al Quds* (the Holy One). Saladin's invitation to the Jews to return brought in a contingent of 300 rabbis from England and France.

Christian and Muslim forces fought for Palestine throughout the 13th century, until the Mamelukes (enfranchised Turkish slaves) took Jerusalem and destroyed coastal cities to remove all potential Crusader footholds.

Ottoman Empire

Palestine remained a backwater for more than 200 years, until it was annexed by the Ottoman Empire in 1516. Suleiman the Magnificent (1520–1566) rebuilt Jerusalem's walls much as you see them today and revived Palestine's industry and agriculture, especially in olive oil.

After the expulsion of Jews from Spain and Portugal, waves of Sephardic immigrants came to Jerusalem and Galilee, especially

Safed and Tiberias. Hundreds of Ashkenazi Jews arrived from Poland in 1700.

Prime Cut
Outside the main cities, Ottoman administration collapsed in the 17th and 18th centuries, leaving the country under the control of local chieftains. One of them, Ahmad Pasha El Jazzar, was in Acre in 1799 when Napoleon Bonaparte arrived fresh from defeat by Admiral Nelson in Egypt. After a fruitless three-month siege, Bonaparte returned to France and left wounded or sick troops to be massacred by El Jazzar—"the Butcher".

In the 19th century, Egypt's Ibrahim Pasha took over Palestine, renewing European interest in the Holy Places. New monasteries, churches, seminaries and hospitals sprang up. Jerusalem became a bone of contention among competing denominations —Greek Orthodox, Armenian, Coptic, Roman Catholic and Protestant. Jewish immigrants also arrived from Central and Eastern Europe, and Hebrew was revived as a modern spoken language.

20th-century Palestine
In 1904, responding to the Zionist movement's call for a Jewish homeland in Palestine, a new wave of immigrants arrived from Russia. Socialists created the first cooperative farms, *kibbutzim,* while other pioneers opted for *moshav,* private enterprise. Tel Aviv was founded in 1909, the first modern Jewish city.

During World War I, amid growing Arab and Jewish rivalry for Palestine, the British played off one side against the other. The Balfour Declaration of 1917 supported a Jewish national home in Palestine. In the same year, after promising independent states to the Arabs if they rose against the Turks, the British defeated the Turkish army and entered Jerusalem. The Arabs found that Palestine, now under British Mandate, was not included among the new independent states. Arab riots in the 1920s and 30s mounted in violence as the rise of Nazism increased the flow of Jewish refugees from Eastern Europe.

In World War II, 30,000 Palestinian Jewish volunteers served with the British Army in North Africa, Europe and Asia.

State of Israel
In 1947, Palestine's 614,000 Jews represented one-third of the population. To give a home to thousands of German concentration camp survivors, the United Nations General Assembly voted to partition the country into independent Arab and Jewish states. This was rejected by the Arabs.

Flashback

On May 14, 1948, the Prime Minister, David Ben Gurion, proclaimed the state of Israel. The next day, Egypt bombed Tel Aviv and the War of Independence began. By January, 1949, the forces of Jordan, Syria, Lebanon, Iraq and Egypt had been routed by Israel's better co-ordinated and, above all, better motivated army.

With eastern Jerusalem, the Jordan's West Bank and Gaza in Arab hands, Israel emerged with 50 per cent more territory than it had accepted by U.N. partition. Anticipating a brief, victorious campaign, Arab leaders had told Palestinian Arabs to leave home temporarily to avoid bloodshed. This left some 400,000 refugees camped in Lebanon, Jordan and Gaza, nurturing resentment not only against Israel but also against their less-than-welcoming hosts.

The 1.5 million newcomers in Israel's first 15 years now included Sephardic Jews from North Africa and Arab countries as well as Ashkenazi European refugees. Frictions between the two had to be overcome in the common effort to create a new nation. A people confined for centuries to roles of craftsmen, commerce and finance now revealed imaginative, innovative talents in agriculture and industry. By geographical necessity, they became world leaders in irrigation and desalination technology. By geopolitical necessity, an army that could not afford to lose wiped out the age-old anti-Semitic image of physical weakness.

War or Peace?

For nearly 50 years, Israel has remained on a permanent war footing. After the War of Independence came the Suez War of 1956, the Six Day War of 1967, the almost disastrous October War of 1973, the Lebanon War of 1982, and more recently Iraq's missile attacks in the Gulf War and the Palestinians' Intifada street war. The need to hold on to conquered territories as bargaining counters for peace created a morale-sapping army of occupation. Peace with Egypt came in 1979 and with Jordan in 1994.

Finding a satisfactory status for the Palestinians is, as Prime Minister Yitzhak Rabin said before shaking hands with their leader Yasser Arafat, "not so easy". For Rabin himself, the effort ended with his assassination by a Jewish extremist in November, 1995. His successors continued the quest for peace—with varying degrees of enthusiasm and success—in public and private diplomacy with the Palestinians and more recalcitrant Syrians. Not so easy, but there was no alternative.

Three Faiths

The three great faiths of monotheism (the belief in one God) impose their presence throughout Israel and Palestine. Let one Jerusalem shrine epitomize the many: the Rock over which the golden Dome is built is honoured by Jews, Christians and Muslims alike as the spot where Abraham prepared to sacrifice his son. It has been further revered by Jews as the rock on which King David set the Ark of the Covenant, the site for Solomon's Temple, and by Muslims as the spot from which Mohammed rose to make his Night Journey to heaven. Here are a few pointers to the three religions.

Judaism

Central to the Jewish religion is the God-given *Torah* (Law). This is generally taken to mean the five books of Moses, but it can refer in its broadest sense to all the Hebrew Scriptures (which Christians call the Old Testament), as well as oral traditions and explanations set down in the books of *Talmud* (Study) and *Midrash* (Investigation). From the Ten Commandments, the Jews' belief in One God forbids any multiple concept like the Christian Trinity or worship of saints. Content with an abstract but nonetheless real idea of God, Judaism tolerates no idolatry and so no image of the deity or, in its place of worship, any human or animal representation. Circumcision of the male child on the eighth day after birth fulfils the divine covenant with Abraham (Genesis 17:10–14). Observation of laws for *kosher* (fit or proper) food forbids the flesh of the pig, shellfish or eating meat and dairy products together. On the Sabbath, from sunset on Friday to sunset on Saturday, the religious Jew refrains from all work. Other holy days include *Rosh Hashana* (New Year), *Yom Kippur* (Day of Atonement), *Succoth* (Tabernacles harvest festival) and *Pesach* (Passover celebrating Exodus from Egypt).

Orthodox Judaism represents the strictest observance of these beliefs and practices. In Israel, it is defined by the Chief Rabbinate, but through *two* Chief Rabbis respectively representing Ashkenazi Jews, largely of German and

Eastern European origin, and Sephardic Jews, from the Arab countries of North Africa and the Middle East. Orthodox fundamentalists live in self-imposed ghettos like Jerusalem's Mea She'arim. Reform Judaism, a movement that spread from 19th-century Germany to America and Britain, is gaining a foothold in Israel with its less fiercely traditionalist, more relaxed, modern interpretation of religion. Unlike Orthodox Judaism, it does not separate men and women in the synagogue and has begun to ordain women rabbis. A third approach, Conservative Judaism, takes a middle road, modernizing its practices while respecting the old traditions.

Islam

The name means in Arabic "submission" to Allah. Islam's book, the Koran (Recitation), covers all features of everyday life, in and outside the mosque—marriage, property, work, eating, drinking and sleeping, as well as prayer. The Koran is Mohammed's presentation in 114 *surahs* (chapters) of Allah's message as he received it from the angel Gabriel. The Allah of the Koran is a loving, just and merciful god. His will determines the lives of all men and women. Their actions on earth determine their place in heaven or hell. The inspired merchant of Mecca (570–632) honoured the Jewish patriarchs and Jesus as pious but fallible prophets. Mohammed as the last prophet had the last word.

In Islam, salvation comes through the five Pillars of Faith. Good Muslims recite each day: "There is no god but Allah, and Mohammed is his prophet." They pray five times a day facing Mecca, and Friday in the mosque. They give alms to the poor and a gift to the mosque. During the month of Ramadan, they observe the fast and other laws of abstinence from dawn to sunset. And at least once, unless they have the dispensation of poverty, they make the pilgrimage to Mecca – the *Hajj*.

Like Judaism's code of what is and is not *kosher*, Islam has religiously determined dietary laws distinguishing *halal* (permitted) from *haram* (forbidden) foods. Circumcision is performed on boys, usually around the age of 10. Though the status of Palestinian women, at least in the cities, is much more egalitarian than in most Islamic communities, they are still excluded from worship with men in the mosques.

The mosque's most prominent feature is of course the minaret, from the top of which the voice of the muezzin calls the faithful to prayer. The mosque is built around a courtyard with a fountain for ritual washing. The main prayer hall faces Mecca as indicated by a niche in the rear wall, the *mihrab*. Other features are a *minbar*, the pulpit from which the Friday sermon is read, and a platform for the imam leading the prayers.

Palestinian Muslims are in their large majority Sunnites, that is to say mainstream believers in a generally more pragmatic interpretation of law based on the words and acts of Mohammed. Shi'ites, regarding the heirs of Mohammed's cousin Ali as true interpreters of the faith, are often the most militant of fundamentalists—a minority in world Islam, but a majority in Iran and Iraq, with sizeable groups in Lebanon and Syria.

Christianity

The most venerated Christian sanctuary in Jerusalem, the Church of the Holy Sepulchre that was the tomb of Jesus Christ, is administered by six denominations—Latin (Roman Catholic), Greek Orthodox, Armenian Orthodox, Coptic, Ethiopian and Syrian. They all accept Jesus as the chosen one, "Christ", whose mission it was to bring salvation to mankind. His death on the Cross was an act of redemption for the sins of all. The idea finds ritual expression in Communion with the wafer of bread and the wine. Fellow Jews resisted the notion that the man from Nazareth was the Son of God and so it was left to apostles Peter and Paul to spread the word among the Gentiles of the Roman Empire, replacing circumcision with baptism. The ranks of the faithful grew until the Roman emperor Constantine was converted in the 4th century. Thereafter, Church councils developed the idea of the Trinity – the unity of Father, Son, and Holy Spirit as three persons in one Godhead. The Church itself divided into East and West, the Greek Orthodoxy of Constantinople and the Catholic papacy of Rome. In turn, Protestants broke with Roman Catholics to emphasize Biblical authority over that of the pope, a more central role for individual free will, greater participation of laymen in the life of the church.

Arab Christians living mainly in Jerusalem, Bethlehem and Nazareth represent only 3 per cent of the total Palestinian population, but many more live in the Palestinian "diaspora". They are mostly members of the Greek Orthodox, Roman Catholic or Melchite Catholic church (observing the Greek rite under Rome's authority). From the US and western Europe, Christian fundamentalists have flocked to Israel hoping to convert the Jews and Muslims or witness the end of the world.

On the Scene

Israel is deceptively tiny, needing a well-planned itinerary to do it justice. Luckily, a first-class road network makes it easy to get around the country, with either Jerusalem or Tel Aviv as your base. In a couple of weeks, you can see something of everything. To combine the "work" of sightseeing with the "play" of lazing on the beach, vary the cities, Holy Places and archaeological sites with time off at the resorts.

JERUSALEM
Old City, Outside the Walls, Modern City Centre, Eastern Jerusalem, Western Outskirts, Excursions

It is enough to make the most hardened atheists believe in a god. The sheer beauty of its setting, the amber light, the rose-hued stone of the buildings, the hills in and around the town touched with the green and silver of the fig and olive trees, might be explanation enough. Of course, none is necessary for religious Jews, Muslims and Christians, drawn here by the city's age-old sanctuaries and traditions. The mystery lies in its effect on others, often provoked to almost angry scepticism by the fervour of devout believers, but feeling nonetheless an equally passionate attachment to the town.

Newcomers can explore these feelings both inside the Old City of David and Solomon, of Mohammed and Jesus, and in the new town that has sprung up outside in the 19th and 20th centuries. The more modern buildings vary in elegance, but they benefit from an imaginative contribution of the British Mandate: the law, still in force, that all exterior construction must use the beautiful Jerusalem stone quarried from the Judaean Hills.

Old City
The massive stone walls look today much as they did after

Built over the Prophet's footprint, Jerusalem's dazzling Dome of the Rock.

OLD CITY

being rebuilt by Turkish Sultan Suleiman the Magnificent in the 16th century. They have eight gates: Jaffa Gate on the west side, leading between the Christian and Armenian Quarters to the Jewish Quarter, two others on the south, two on the east, and three on the north, including Damascus Gate for the Muslim Quarter.

Tower of David

Your ideal introduction to the Old City starts here, immediately inside Jaffa Gate. The city's 3,000-year-old history is beautifully presented on the site of a citadel built by Herod in c. 24 BC, but impressive enough for early Christian pilgrims to attribute it to King David. The sturdy fortifications you see now are largely the work of the 14th-century Mamelukes, forming a dramatic backdrop for Sound and Light shows performed from March to November. The story of Jerusalem is presented in audio-visual displays tastefully arranged around an archaeological courtyard and pleasant garden café. Excavated artefacts include Canaanite pottery, bricks inscribed with Roman graffiti, Arab invaders' catapult stones, Crusader arms and armour and Ottoman hookah pipes. A major feature is a scale model of the city executed in zinc by a Hungarian artisan in 1873.

Jaffa Gate

Built in 1531 by Suleiman the Magnificent, this terminus of the 19th-century road linking Jerusalem with the port of Jaffa is known to Arabs as *Bab el Khalil* (Hebron Gate). Leading straight from the gate, on David Street, are colourful shops selling car-

---

THE TWO BEST CITY TOURS An easy way to take in a maximum of city landmarks is **Bus No. 99** which passes 34 different sightseeing points on a 90-minute journey. This Circular Line starts out from Jerusalem Central Bus Station, but you can pick it up more centrally at Jaffa Gate—four daily tours Sunday to Thursday, two on Friday. On foot, the **Ramparts Tour** gives you a splendid rooftop view of the Old City. Best starting point is Damascus Gate, head west atop the wall past the Christian Quarter to Jaffa Gate and on around the Armenian and Jewish Quarters to the Temple Mount.

pets, embroidery, brassware, inlay, onyx, *menorah* candelabras, wood-carvings, mother-of-pearl, T-shirts, good stuff and junk, but also market-stalls and barrows of fruit, nuts, vegetables and spices.

Jewish Quarter

Right off David Street, ancient Cardo Street, part Roman, part Byzantine, has been restored to house modern galleries and boutiques under the arches and colonnades. The neighbourhood is also inhabited by the families of rabbis and their *Yeshiva* (theological) students, for whom imposing modern seminaries have been built. Many important synagogues, destroyed under the Jordanian occupation after 1948, have been restored. Ashkenazi Jews originating from Germany and Eastern Europe worshipped at the Hurva Synagogue, of which all that remains is a stone arch. Sephardic descendants of the Spanish expulsion have four older synagogues grouped together: the Johanan Ben Zakkai (built where the revered rabbi taught in the days of the Second Temple), Eliahu HaNavi, Istambuli and Em'tzai.

Western Wall

Since the triumphant reunification of Jerusalem in 1967, Jews have abandoned the notion of a "wailing wall" after centuries of lamenting Roman destruction of the Second Temple in AD 70. But the last surviving visible structure of the sanctuary, on the west side of Temple Mount, remains a no less hallowed place of prayer for the devout—and revered by non-religious Jews as a symbol of their historic roots. The plaza sloping down to the wall holds up to 100,000 people. They pray in separate groups according to their different traditions. To approach the wall itself, men must don a prayer-cap (provided at the entrance to the enclosure); there's a separate section for women, modestly dressed. It is the custom to place a written prayer between the huge ashlar stones of the wall (the papers are taken out once a month and buried in consecrated ground).

Temple Tunnel

Beneath an arch at the north end of the exposed portion of the Western Wall are vaulted chambers dating back in part to the temple's pre-Herodian era of the Hasmoneans (Maccabees). They form a passage meeting up with a tunnel that runs north beyond the Temple Mount to emerge at the Via Dolorosa. The controversial excavations completed in 1996 caused riots in the Palestinian community who feared the tunnel would endanger foundations of the El-Aqsa Mosque. In fact, the

OLD CITY

tunnel runs outside the Muslim sanctuary and has existed for centuries; the new excavations involve only the Via Dolorosa exit.

On guided tours, you can see an ancient *mikva* (ritual bath), Roman stone ammunition used in the Jewish revolt of 135 AD, and a synagogue of the 8th century AD built round one of the arches of a Temple gate. A scale model shows in great detail what the Second Temple probably looked like. How the Temple coped with the eternal problem of Jerusalem's water supply can be seen in the Hasmoneans' cisterns and aqueduct.

Dome of the Rock

As hallowed for Muslims as the Western Wall is for Jews, the *Qubbet es-Sakhra* was built on Temple Mount in 691 over the rock from which Mohammed is said to have made a night journey to pray in heaven with Abraham, Moses and Jesus. The belief derives from a verse in the Koran: "Praise be to Allah who brought his servant at night from the Holy Mosque to the Far Away Mosque, the precincts of which we have blessed." The great dome, brilliantly regilded by Jordan's King Hussein in 1993, has become the landmark symbol for

---

VIA DOLOROSA

The route that Jesus took to his Crucifixion runs through the middle of the Muslim Quarter, starting out on Lion's Gate Street east of El Wad. Daily at 3 p.m., Franciscan monks lead a procession to the 14 Stations of the Cross which combine fact with traditional legend.

1. *Court of Jesus' condemnation by Pontius Pilate* in Antonia Fortress, now part of El-Omariye School;
2. *Flagellation, Crown of Thorns and Cross* given to Jesus in courtyard of Franciscan Monastery of the Flagellation;
3. *Falls first time* under weight of Cross, marked by a Polish chapel;
4. *Meets mother Mary*, shrine at Armenian church of Our Lady of the Spasm;
5. *Simon helps carry the Cross*—19th-century Franciscan chapel;
6. *Veronica wipes his face* leaving True Image on cloth—church in Crusader monastery;
7. *Falls second time*—Via Dolorosa crosses Khan es-Zeit market street;
8. *Tells women not to weep*—marked by cross and Greek inscription NIKA;
9. *Falls third time*—column in wall of Ethiopian church;
10.–14. *Climb to Calvary*, inside Church of Holy Sepulchre.

the whole city. The decoration of the octagonal mosque's interior of marble and coloured tiles is an equally splendid blend of Koranic verses with arabesque and floral patterns. Remove your shoes before entering.

El-Aqsa Mosque
The silver-domed shrine at the south end of Temple Mount was originally built in the 8th century, from which time only a mosaic floor survives. The "furthest spot" mentioned in its name is where Mohammed stopped on his ride from Medina to Jerusalem before his miraculous night journey. The largest mosque in Jerusalem, it suffered the indignities of earthquake and transformation by the Crusaders into a residence and church before Saladin reclaimed it for Islam in 1187. It has been restored with massive marble pillars and handsome Oriental carpets.

Damascus Gate
Known to the Hebrews as *Sha'ar Shechem* (Nablus Gate), this monumental entrance to the Muslim Quarter and its bustling bazaar is Suleiman the Magnificent's Jerusalem masterpiece. It stands above the galleries of a recently excavated Roman bastion, now the Roman Gate Museum. East of the gate is a cave identified as Solomon's Quarries for the stone that built the First Temple. Immediately inside the gate are the money-changers, among whom an ever-smiling Arab Christian lady named Victoria is a veritable institution.

The Souk (Arab Bazaar)
The Muslim Quarter's bazaar is a cluster of narrow alleys and vaulted passages around El Wad, the main street leading to the Temple Mount. With its hookah smokers at the little cafés, colourful displays of fruit, nuts and spices, of mutton and poultry, jewellery and brassware, it is the most emphatically "Middle Eastern" spot in all Jerusalem.

Church of St Anne
Near Lion's Gate in the eastern wall is Jerusalem's finest Crusader church, built over the home of Mary's parents, St Anne and St Joachim. In this Catholic church, a splendid piece of Burgundian Romanesque architecture (1142), you can visit the grotto where Mary is said to have been born.

Church of Holy Sepulchre
Byzantine Emperor Constantine built the original church in 335 on the site that his mother Helena had identified nine years earlier as that of the Crucifixion on Calvary. The first great edifice was destroyed by the Persians in 614. It was rebuilt and destroyed again

OLD CITY • OUTSIDE THE WALLS

Skull-capped scholars poring over the Torah beside the Western Wall.

many times throughout the Crusades and subsequent wars between Muslims and Christians. Entrance is through the Crusaders' western façade, which retains its Romanesque grandeur. Otherwise, the present hybrid structure faithfully reflects the rival claims of the six Christian denominations vying for control of the sanctuary. The nave is Greek Orthodox. The choir and southern section of Calvary rock are Roman Catholic. The east chapel of the ambulatory dedicated to the three Maries (Virgin, Magdalene and mother of James) is Armenian Orthodox, while other shrines are administered by the Copts, the Abyssinians and Syrians. The Stone of Unction, where Jesus' body was anointed, and the Rotunda over the Holy Sepulchre are the only two sites administered jointly by all denominations.

Outside the Walls

Immediately adjacent to the Old City's ramparts are sites closely associated with Biblical Jerusalem. It makes sense to combine a visit to these with your tour of the Old City.

Mount of Olives

To visit the historic hill overlooking Temple Mount, take a bus or taxi to the top and walk down—or ride a camel. The highest point is the 19th-century tower of the Russian Orthodox church of the Ascension, identified by its clergy as the place from which Jesus made his journey to heaven (the church is open only by special permission). A little lower down, within the precincts of a small mosque, is the octagonal Chapel of the Ascension that marks the sacred spot for other denominations.

One of the best views of the city can be had from the terrace in front of the Seven Arches Hotel. Below the hotel are the Tombs of the Prophets—tunnels of burial niches attributed, among others, to Haggai and Malachi. Olive trees still grow among the ancient tombs, most evocatively of all in the Garden of Gethsemane where Jesus spent his last hours before being arrested by the Romans. Among the many modern churches on the lower slopes are the seven-domed Russian Orthodox church of Mary Magdalene and the Greek Orthodox church of the Assumption, built over an earlier Crusader church housing Mary's rock-hewn sepulchre.

Valley of Kidron
Running south between the Mount of Olives and the Temple Mount, the valley is the site of many tombs from the Biblical era. One is attributed to David's son, Absalom, and a smaller one behind it to Jehoshaphat, king of Judah.

Ongoing excavations have uncovered remains of the City of David, scarcely more than a village, the tunnel of Gihon Spring, and further south, the Pool of Siloam, both vital sources of water for parched Jerusalem.

Mount Zion
This hill southwest of the Old City is steeped in Biblical history. Its most prominent landmark is the imposing modern Benedictine abbey church of the Dormition (1910), built over a crypt where Mary is believed to have begun her dying sleep. Across from the church is the Tomb of David and above it, the Coenaculum (dining-room) where Jesus is said to have eaten his Last Supper.

Modern City Centre
West Jerusalem has recently perked up with lively bars, open-air cafés, good restaurants and brighter shops. It's still not Manhattan, but the town does have a new bounce to it.

Around Ben Yehuda Street
Zion Square is the heart of the main shopping district along the busy Jaffa Road. From here, the pedestrian zone of Ben Yehuda Street climbs past ice-cream par-

MODERN CITY CENTRE

lours, falafel stalls and souvenir shops. Street musicians abound, many of astounding quality, straight from the academies of St Petersburg and Moscow. The quaint houses of the nearby renovated Nakhalat Shiv'a neighbourhood have been converted into bars, nightclubs and kosher spaghetti houses. In the evening, especially Saturday after the Sabbath, the place is invaded by the young crowd.

Makhane Yehuda

At the top of Jaffa Street, West Jerusalem's main market pays boisterous tribute to Israel's cosmopolitan origins with its rich variety of fruit and vegetables, spices, meat and fish. On the eve of Sabbath and other holidays, it's a joyous bedlam in which the Orthodox and secular drown their weekday differences. There are some great little restaurants in the Kurdish-Iraqi neighbourhood along Agrippas Street.

Russian Compound

North of Jaffa Road, behind the attractive new City Hall, is the green-domed Russian Orthodox cathedral. In the 19th century, it was the centre of a Russian community of clergy, functionaries and pilgrims. Bought by the Israeli government, the complex houses the police headquarters, a jail and courthouse. On the north side of the compound, Kol Israel state radio and television occupies a rambling mansion belonging to the Ethiopian Church.

King David Street

The massive landmark of the King David Hotel, built in 1930, has been home to many chiefs of state, royal and otherwise, and countless ruinously spoiled *barmitzvah* boys, Jewish-American princesses and their parents. In 1946, as the British Mandate's political and military headquarters, it was the target of a right-wing Jewish terrorist bomb that killed 91 British, Arabs and Jews. Across the road is the YMCA hotel, another 1930s building with a magnificent view from the top of its imposing Moorish-Islamic tower and a pleasant café on the terrace at street level.

East of the King David Hotel, there's a pleasant promenade and park that includes the Herodian Tomb, a Moroccan garden with fountains and the Montefiore windmill (which serves as a museum), overlooking the Old City ramparts. At the foot of the promenade is the new residential and artists' quarter, Yemin Moshe.

Mea She'arim and Bukhara

Since the 1870s, ultra-Orthodox Jews have gathered in these two unchanging neighbourhoods north of the Russian Compound.

They continue the style of life their ancestors led in the 18th-century Hasidic communities of Eastern Europe and among the pious Uzbeks of Bukhara. Bearded with side-whiskers in *peyer* ringlets, the Hasidic men wear broad-brimmed hats, long frock-coats and leggings, while the women wear long dresses, concealing their shorn hair beneath wigs. They combine strict religious observance and study with a joyful celebration of their faith in song and dance—and usually have lots of children. Visitors to these neighbourhoods should dress with modesty.

Eastern Jerusalem

The Arab part of the city, Muslim and Christian, is appreciated for its hospitable shopkeepers and fine restaurants, many of them with evening entertainment. Keep in mind that shops here (but not restaurants) close for the Muslim Sabbath from Thursday sunset to Friday sunset. The neighbourhood stretching north and east of the Old City's Damascus Gate includes several Christian and Jewish monuments.

Garden Tomb

Hewn from the rock in a garden off the Nablus Road *(Derekh Shekhem),* this tomb dates back to Roman times. It is tended by an association of Anglican Protestants sharing the theory of its discoverer, British General Charles Gordon of Khartoum, that this, not the Holy Sepulchre, is the burial place of Jesus.

American Colony Hotel

Further out on the Nablus Road, this was once the residence of a Turkish pasha. With its lovely gardens for afternoon tea, it's as much an institution in Arab Jerusalem as the King David over in the west. But where the latter has courted princes and presidents, the American Colony has been the favoured haunt of actors and writers, from Peter O'Toole and Peter Ustinov to Saul Bellow and Graham Greene—and also bigwigs of the PLO.

The "colony" of the surrounding neighbourhood takes its name from American philanthropists of the 19th century.

Rockefeller Museum

On Sultan Suleiman Street, opposite the northeast corner of the Old City, this important museum of antiquities was funded by John D. Rockefeller. Its exhibits include the remains of Palestine's earliest prehistoric inhabitants, artefacts from the Biblical cities of Megiddo and Beth She'an, mosaic floors of ancient synagogues, together with splendid examples of Islamic art from 8th-century Jericho and Jerusalem.

EASTERN JERUSALEM • WESTERN OUTSKIRTS

Mount Scopus
The view of the city and Judaean Hills makes the ride worthwhile, best of all from the amphitheatre where open-air concerts are held in the summer. Since 1967, the Hebrew University campus has been restored and extended; it is most notable for the Harry Truman Research Institute and the renovated Hadassah Hospital designed in 1936 by German architect Erich Mendelsohn.

Western Outskirts
Extensive parks surround the museums and parliament buildings overlooking the city.

Israel Museum
From modest beginnings in 1965 as a patriotic assemblage of Israeli and Jewish art and artefacts, the museum has blossomed into one of the major artistic and archaeological collections of the Mediterranean. A village of white stone and glass buildings houses the prehistoric, Biblical, Islamic and other works from around the world.

The major attraction is the Shrine of the Book, housing the 2,000-year-old Dead Sea Scrolls. Beneath a flattened dome resembling a lid of the clay jars in which they were found in 1947, fragile but clearly legible Hebrew scrolls of the Psalms and book of Isaiah are displayed in a special climatically controlled atmosphere. The archaeological collections (c. 4000 BC) include ivory statuettes from Beersheba and the spectacular Judaean Desert Treasure of crowns, sceptres and maces uncovered at Ein Gedi. From Biblical times, you can see King Ahab's gateway capital from Galilee, a reassembled Judaean sanctuary from Arad, a seal of Nebuchadnezzar, a limestone inscription of Pontius Pilate from Caesarea, and ancient mosaic floors from post-Second Temple synagogues.

Modern art is represented by the painting of Europe and the Americas and a sculpture garden that includes Rodin, Picasso and Henry Moore.

Bible Lands Museum
Adjacent to the Israel Museum, this is a popular collection specifically linked to the Bible. Artefacts from ancient Israel, Egypt, Babylon and the early Christian world of Byzantium illustrate episodes in the Old and New Testaments in chronological order from 6000 BC to AD 600.

Knesset and Supreme Court
Free guided tours in English are offered around these major buildings of Israeli government, off Ruppin Boulevard (bring your passport). In front of the Knesset stands a monumental bronze

menorah (candelabra) offered by the "mother of parliaments", the British House of Commons. The star attraction is the world's most free-wheeling, open-necked, even T-shirted, debating chamber—a great show even if you don't speak a word of Hebrew. If numbers allow, you may gain access to the Visitors' Gallery while parliament is in session.

Architecturally more impressive is the new Supreme Court designed in 1992 by Ram and Ada Karmi, with a pleasant terrace overlooking Jerusalem and the Judaean Hills.

Yad Vashem

This memorial to the victims and survivors of the German concentration camps is an essential part of any visit to Jerusalem for anyone wanting to understand Israel in the context of the 20th century. In a peaceful garden setting near Mount Herzl, the presentation is simple and eloquent: an Avenue of the Righteous pays tribute with over 500 trees planted in the name of Gentiles who risked their lives to save the Jews of Europe; a Hall of Remembrance names the camps with a flame burning to honour the dead; a Hall of Names records over 3 million victims so far identified; a monument commemorates the million and a half children; a Historical Museum documents the facts.

Excursions

The hills and valleys around Jerusalem are green with new forests, orchards and vineyards or ochre with the tones of the Judaean desert. They make any excursion a refreshing change from the city. It is possible to take a guided tour of kibbutz communities such as Zova, just 20 minutes from town.

Ein Kerem

This exquisite village on the western outskirts of Jerusalem is believed to be the birthplace of John the Baptist. A 17th-century church is built over the saint's grotto, bearing the Latin inscription *Hic Praecursor Domini natus est*, "Here was born the Precursor of the Lord". A modern church built over a Crusader edifice is dedicated to the visit of Mary to her cousin Elisabeth.

Abu Gosh

Ten kilometres (6 miles) west along the highway towards Tel Aviv is the attractive Arab Muslim village founded by an 18th-century Bedouin sheikh licensed by the Ottoman authorities to collect tolls from travellers heading for Jerusalem. Descendants still living there content themselves with the income from the tourist restaurants. A superb example of Crusader church architecture was rebuilt by French Benedictine monks.

WILDERNESS AND DESERT
Judaean Wilderness, Dead Sea, Negev

After just a 40-minute ride from Jerusalem, the sparkle of the Dead Sea can be seen from the hillside suburbs on the road to Jericho, with the Jordanian hills of Moab on the eastern horizon.

Judaean Wilderness

The Arab towns of the Judaean Wilderness are as rich in ancient and Biblical history as Jerusalem itself. As the peace process has progressed, they have gradually been brought under Palestinian administration.

Under normal circumstances, you will find Palestinians naturally warm, hospitable and eager to promote their tourist industry. (Tour groups advise on varying security conditions in the West Bank's Occupied Territories. Be sure to travel with your passport.)

Jericho

The world's oldest city, founded around 8300 BC, is also the lowest, 250 m (820 ft) below sea level, less than an hour's drive northeast of Jerusalem. Its plentiful springs make it a veritable oasis in the Judaean desert with gardens full of greenery, bougain-

Modern-day miracle: swimming pool in the desert at Ein Gedi.

villaea and other vivid flowers. What Joshua's trumpets didn't blow down was smashed through the ages in the Revolt against the Romans of Hadrian and the wars of Muslims and Crusaders. The town lay in semi-abandon until the 19th century.

On the outskirts are three sights worth visiting: to the north, the ruin of the 8th-century Caliph Hisham's Palace, toppled by an earthquake; St George's Monastery inhabited by Greek Orthodox monks on the side of the Wadi Qilt ravine west of town; and to the northwest, on Temptation Mount, the Monastery of the Forty Days, built by the Russian Orthodox church over the spot where Jesus fasted 40 days rather than yield to Satan.

Bethlehem

Jesus' birthplace is now a largely Christian Arab city (population 25,000) just 7 km (4 miles) south of Jerusalem. The Old Testament mentions it as *Bet-Lehem* (House of Bread) while the subsequent Arab name became *Beit-Lahm* (House of Meat).

At the north edge of town, the Tomb of Rachel, wife of the patriarch Jacob, is a place of pilgrimage for devout Jews, Muslims and Christians, particularly women praying for a baby. Hub of the city is Manger Square, bustling with peddlers of religious souvenirs in mother-of-pearl, wood and black basalt.

Nearby, the Church of the Nativity stands over the sacred grotto identified in 326 by Helena, mother of Emperor Constantine. The present edifice is essentially a 6th-century church built by Emperor Justinian after the original was destroyed by Samaritan rebels. Like the Holy Sepulchre, its administration is shared by Greek Orthodox, Armenian, Roman Catholic and Protestant clergy. Each sect takes care of one part of the church, but in practice this has no effect on visitors, who can wander at will.

Hebron

Home and burial place of Abraham, Isaac and Jacob, this Arab city in the Judaean Hills, 36 km (22 miles) south of Jerusalem, has been a focus of recent Israeli-Palestinian conflict.

In peaceful times, Jews and Muslims pray separately at the site of the Cave of Machpelah, identified as the tomb of the patriarchs and their wives Sarah, Rebecca and Leah. The beautifully decorated mosque over the cave, Haram el-Khalil (Shrine of the Friend), dates back to a 2,000-year-old structure from the age of Herod.

Dead Sea

This 80-km (50-mile) stretch of water (17 km/10 miles at its widest point) is one of the wonders of the Middle East. It is the lowest point on earth, 398 m (1,305 ft) below the level of any normal sea. The hot desert air evaporates freshwater inflow from the Jordan river too fast for living organisms to survive in what seems to any human swimmer like a huge bowl of salt soup. Ten times saltier than the Mediterranean Sea, it will make you lick your lips with thirst, even at first sight.

No fish here, not even rollmops, but plenty of minerals—besides abundant table salt, industrial potassium, bromide and magnesium. The people who exploit these minerals at the Dead Sea Works live in the southern town of Sedom, the successor community of Biblical Sodom and Gomorrah, but much better behaved.

Qumran

The barren Judaean hills plunging down to the Dead Sea's northwest shore provided a refuge for the Jewish sect of Essenes at the time of the Second Temple. It was here, in the caves of Qumran, that they hid from the approaching Roman army their manuscripts of the Old Testament and other inspirational writings—the famous Dead Sea Scrolls. Today you can visit the excavated houses of their 2,000-year-old community and see, if not penetrate, the caves where the scrolls were found by two Bedouin goatherds in 1947.

Ein Gedi

In this most beautiful of green oases fed by a cascade of freshwater springs (*Ein Gedi* means Fountain of the Kid), read King Solomon's *Song of Songs*. For this is where the wise and passionate man came to woo a Shulamite maiden: "My beloved is to me a cluster of camphire in the vineyards of Ein Gedi."

In the present-day nature park organized by the local kibbutz, you will find the fig trees, pomegranates, apples and palm trees of Solomon's poem, as well as the gazelles, mountain goats, leopards and hyenas that roamed the desert in Biblical times. A stalactite cave near the waterfall is said to be the place where David had a famous confrontation with King Saul.

The beach here is also a good place to take your dip in the Dead Sea. Swimmers and non-swimmers alike can't help floating—in fact it is much easier to float than to swim—but afterwards be sure to use one of the beach showers, preferably twice, to get rid of the salt.

Masada

Both by its awesome history and by its isolated location in the Judaean desert 18 km (11 miles) south of Ein Gedi, the fortress of Masada is one of the most dramatic sites in Israel. It is built on a sheer-sided flat-topped hill 450 m (1,476 ft) above the Dead

THREE OASES provide refreshment in the great wildernesses of the Judaean and Negev deserts. Transformed into a nature park, the rich greenery of **Ein Gedi** lies at the edge of the Judaean desert on the Dead Sea. The colourful flowers and trees of **Jericho** nestling deep in a valley of the Judaean Hills make it clear that the oldest city in the world began life as a resting place for desert nomads. **En Avdat** is a beautiful spring in the Negev hills between David Ben Gurion's kibbutz at Sede Boqer and remains of the great Nabatean-Byzantine town of Avdat.

Sea. Expanded by Herod on a grand scale from a more modest Maccabee redoubt, it was seized from the Romans in the Jewish Revolt of AD 70. When its defences were breached three years later, zealot leaders set fire to the fortress and 960 men, women and children committed collective suicide by the sword, rather than submit to Roman slavery. Two women and five children survived to tell the tale. Modern Israelis honour the heroic resistance and, if they differ on the significance of the sacrifice, are unanimous in the slogan: "Never again, Masada."

Today, the route to the top is either by cable car to a stairway of 80 steps or an hour's easy-going walk up the original Snake Path. The easiest solution is to ride up and walk back down. In any case, be sure to guard against dehydration by drinking plenty of water on the way and at the top—drinking water and toilet facilities are available both at the park-entrance and on the archaeological site.

The Masada of Herod is a true royal citadel with two palaces, villas, synagogue, storerooms, bathhouse, swimming pool and water cisterns. On your way to the fine three-terraced Northern Palace, you pass the so-called Lottery Area. Here, 11 ostraca (potsherds) were found bearing names of those leaders who drew lots to carry out the collective suicide. A 50-minute Sound and Light show narrates the historic events in a specially built open-air theatre facing the Roman invasion-ramp, with simultaneous headphone-translation in English, French, German, Spanish and Russian.

En Boqeq

This holiday resort is conveniently close at hand for overnight visitors to Masada. Its seafront hotels have good beaches in addition to health spa facilities that specialize in the famous Dead Sea mud baths.

The Negev

West of Masada, the Negev desert begins, stretching south to the Egyptian border of the Sinai peninsula. It covers fully 60 per cent of Israel's land surface, in which new industrial development towns like Arad and Dimona and experimental desert-farms are gradually replacing the military camps. Organized excursions giving a first taste of the desert take three or four days.

Beersheba

The Negev's capital once marked the southern boundary of Biblical Israel. A burgeoning new university town has sprung up at the site where the patriarchs Abraham

THE NEGEV

In the salty soup of the Dead Sea, it's easier to float than to stand up.

and Isaac made a covenant with the Negev's King Abimelech and where Bedouins still bring their camels to market (now every Thursday morning). The Ben Gurion University holds open-air concerts, and a modest museum exhibits the region's archaeological finds.

Sede Boqer

Some 40 km (25 miles) south of Beersheba is the kibbutz where David Ben Gurion spent his last years, now a celebrated centre for desert research. The simple home and library of Israel's first prime minister have been turned into a museum. Nearby, his grave, together with that of his wife Paula, overlooks the stunningly beautiful wilderness.

Avdat

South of Sede Boqer lie the remains of a great Nabatean city, at the crossroads of the ancient Jerusalem–Eilat route and the desert to coast route from Petra to Gaza. The Nabateans, a kingdom of semi-nomadic Arabs, flourished from trade for 500 years, until their conquest by the Romans in AD 106. Burial caves and remains of their pottery kiln and workshops share the site with Roman houses, a Byzantine fortress and two churches.

GALILEE
Tiberias, Sea of Galilee, Safed, Nazareth

The green and pleasant land around the Sea of Galilee is closely associated with the life of Jesus, his miracles and disciples. Jewish sages sought refuge here in Tiberias after the destruction of the Second Temple, as well as in Safed in the 16th century, after their expulsion from Spain. Between times, the hilly country was a battleground in the Crusades against the Muslims, marked today by the ruined castles left by the Christian knights.

The waters are those that Jesus is said to have walked on. The large lake-perch known here as St Peter's fish is served in lakeside restaurants, though they cannot claim to feed 5,000 customers with just a couple of them. But the natural beauty and peace of the place are still an inspiration for the pilgrims who come here. Daily cruises are available to take you between the resort of Tiberias on the west shore across to the charming kibbutz of En Gev on the east, or north to Peter's birthplace at Capernaum.

The more mountainous Upper Galilee north of the lake is separated from the rolling country of Lower Galilee by the Bet Kerem Valley, through which a major highway runs from Safed to Acre on the coast.

Tiberias

Today a thriving beach resort on the lake's west shore, the 2,000-year-old town was founded by Herod's son and dedicated to Roman emperor Tiberius. It is one of the four Jewish holy cities —with Jerusalem, Hebron and Safed. During their refuge here when Palestine was under Roman and Byzantine rule, rabbinic scholars prepared a Talmudic compilation of Jewish law and tradition and a definitive Hebrew version of the Old Testament. They were followed by Spanish Jews in the 16th century and Hasidic communities from Eastern Europe in the 18th.

Its atmosphere now is more emphatically secular, with tourists flocking to the modern hotels to enjoy the mellow climate, hot spring cures, good fish restaurants, pleasant beach and cruises on the lake.

Tomb of Maimonides

In the ancient Jewish cemetery on Johanan Ben Zakkai Street is the burial place of the man whom many regard as Judaism's greatest post-Biblical scholar. Also respectfully known as Rambam, a Hebraic abbreviation of *R*abbi *M*oses *B*en *M*aimon, the Spanish philosopher died in 1204 in Cairo where he had served as Saladin's court physician. Maimonides attracts to his tomb a veritable cult of admirers of his masterwork, *Guide for the Perplexed,* a still relevant rational interpretation of the Bible, written in Arabic. Other great rabbis from the town's scholarly past are buried nearby.

St Peter's Crusader Church
Restored by Franciscan monks in the 19th century, the lakeside church was originally built by the Crusaders with a keel-like apse beyond the nave to recall the boat of fisherman Peter. The Franciscan cloisters are an attractive place for a moment of peace.

Hot Springs
Just south of town are the Turkish baths, Hammath Tiberias, whose healing waters have attracted the ailing and merely bone-weary since ancient Roman times. The springs gushing forth at a temperature of up to 65 °C (149 °F) are said to be particularly good for skin disorders; however, pilgrims and tourists over the last 2,000 years also swear by their curative powers for the dreaded disease of "sightseeing feet". The present installations are ultra-modern, but ask to see the ornate vaulted pool built by Ibrahim Pasha of Egypt.

Across the road is a museum devoted to the ancient baths and, on the hill just above, controversial mosaics from a 4th-century synagogue. Together with the holy ark between two seven-branched *menorah* candelabras, the mosaic depicts, contrary to Jewish religious law, the 12 astrological signs of the Zodiac encircling the Greek sun-god Helios.

Sea of Galilee
Measuring 21 km (13 miles) in length and an average of 12 km (7 miles) in width, the lake is Israel's principal source of fresh water, for which a Natural Water Carrier was built in 1964 to pipe it all the way south to the Negev desert. It is in large part the protection of this precious resource, 4 thousand million cubic metres of fresh water, that has made the Golan Heights overlooking the lake's eastern shores a perennial bone of contention between Israel and Syria.

En Gev
A frequent boat-service from Tiberias takes you across to this kibbutz on the east shore. It is worth a visit both for its pleasant little beach and the restaurant, where you can sample St Peter's fish—caught increasingly in the Jordan River to supplement heavy demand on the lake's resources. With the Golan Heights looming behind it, the kibbutz itself is an interesting example of

Sea of Galilee

> **GOSPEL TRUTH**
>
> In the New Testament, St Matthew calls it the Sea of Galilee (favoured by English-speaking Christians). St John prefers the Sea of Tiberias (adopted by the French as *Tibériade*), while Luke proposes the Lake of Gennesaret (favoured, as *Genezareth,* by the Germans). For Jews ancient and modern, the Old Testament calls it the Lake of *Kinneret* (lyre or harp), seeing the lake shaped like King David's favourite musical instrument.

eastern Galilee's farming and fishing communities, regularly shelled by Syrian artillery until the Six Day War in 1967.

Tabgha

The road north of Tiberias winds through beautiful lakeside country, passing to the west Mount Hattin, identified as the place where St Matthew describes Jesus' Sermon on the Mount (according to Luke, Jesus "stood in the plain"). At Tabgha—from the Greek *Heptapegon,* Seven Springs, in Hebrew *En Sheva*—is the 20th-century Church of Multiplication. It stands over an earlier, 4th-century church marking the stone slab where Jesus multiplied the loaves and fishes to feed the 5,000 people gathered to hear him. There are splendid ancient mosaics depicting the flora and fauna of the lake.

Capernaum

On the lake's northwest shore, accessible from Tiberias both by road or by boat, is the place of St Peter's birth and where Jesus assembled his disciples after moving here from Nazareth. (Its Hebrew name is *Kefar Nahum,* village of Nahum, perhaps the Jewish prophet.) Once a busy fishing port, the archaeological site has revealed remains of houses from Jesus' time and a handsome white limestone Synagogue (3rd century AD) with richly carved pillars. Franciscan monks have identified an ancient octagonal church erected around 450 over the house of St Peter, now under a concrete roof.

Belvoir

Sixteen kilometres (10 miles) south of the Sea of Galilee, this hilltop Crusader castle, a noble ruin but one of the best preserved in Israel, makes a fine excursion for travellers coming to or from Jerusalem. Built in the 12th century but later dismantled by the Muslims fearing a new Crusader invasion, an inner fortress of black basalt is enclosed by pentagonal ramparts with watchtowers surveying the Jordan Valley. The view is magnificent.

Bet She'an

This ancient city stands at the junction of the Jezreel and Jordan Valleys, 26 km (16 miles) south of the Sea of Galilee. It was a major town of transit between Damascus and the Mediterranean road to Egypt, the *Via Maris*. Occupied without interruption for 5,000 years, its modern town is inhabited largely by Jews from North Africa. The ancient site is a fine example of archaeological excavation, revealing eighteen levels of occupation from prehistoric times to the arrival of the Arabs in the 7th century AD. Monuments include remains of Egyptian temples and palaces, Roman villas, baths and a superb theatre originally seating 8,000 spectators, and two Samaritan synagogues.

Safed (Zefat)

Beautifully situated high on Mount Canaan in Upper Galilee, this town 35 km (21 miles) north of Tiberias can justly call itself the capital of Jewish mysticism. With Jerusalem, Hebron and Tiberias, it is considered one of the four Jewish holy cities. But at 900 m (2,952 ft) above sea level, the town benefits from a bracing climate and extraordinary luminosity that have attracted a colony of artists decidedly less pious than the rabbinical scholars with whom they coexist.

Fortified by leaders of the Jewish Revolt, the town, like Tiberias, received its first sages after the destruction of the Second Temple in AD 70. It dropped out of history until it became a Crusader citadel in the 12th century and passed back and forth between Christians and Muslims. Leading Kabbalist sages were among the Spanish Jews who arrived after the Turkish conquest in 1516. Their mysticism was renewed in the 18th century by

KABBALAH, A MATTER OF QUESTION

The kabbalah (literally "reception") is often regarded as an occult dogma perpetuated by a secret society of abracadabrists twisting dark, bizarre interpretations from sacred texts. Mystical it certainly is, in the sense of seeking meanings that surpass or probe beneath ordinary human understanding. But there is nothing dogmatic about true kabbalists, experiencing a revival in modern Israel. Elaborated first in France in the 11th century and then in Spain, their approach to texts does not impose one sense at the expense of another. In fact, when asked why they always answer every question with another question, kabbalists reply: "Why not?"

Hasidic rabbis from Eastern Europe, but disease, earthquake and war decimated the population. In 1948, the town's strategic location provoked a fierce battle for the citadel, and the majority Arab population fled after the Israeli victory.

Citadel

Before you are tired out by your Old Town tour, climb up to the remains of the Crusader castle set in a pleasant park. It affords a splendid view of the city and the surrounding countryside.

The Synagogues

The Old Town quarter huddled beneath the Citadel has countless synagogues, most looking like ordinary houses. To find the main synagogues dedicated to the great scholars in the warren of narrow streets, you need a guided tour by someone who knows the town inside out. The tourist information office tells you the only one is "God", but some others can help you. The most important are the two Ha-Ari synagogues, one Sephardic, one Ashkenazi, honouring Kabbalist master Isaac Luria, nicknamed *Ha-Ari* (The Lion); the Joseph Caro Synagogue named for the fine Kabbalist writer from Toledo; and the Abouav, preserving the great rabbi's own 15th-century Scrolls of the Law.

Beit Hameiri Folk Museum

A group of little old houses of the Hameiri family dates back to 1517, having miraculously survived centuries of earthquake and fire to present a view of Jewish community life in Safed at the end of the 19th century: costumes, furniture, kitchen utensils, household ornaments, machinery and tools.

Ethiopian Folk Art Centre

Craftwork on display in the Synagogue Quarter has been created by artists among the Ethiopian Jews clandestinely airlifted into Israel in the 1980s Operation Moses.

Jewish Cemetery

At the northwest corner of town are the 16th-century tombs of Isaac Luria, Joseph Caro and other rabbis. Nearby are the modern graves of soldiers killed in the battle for Safed in 1948.

Artists' Quarter

South of the Citadel, galleries and studios for some 50 painters and sculptors have been installed in what was formerly the Arab quarter of town. The mosque serves now as a communal gallery. The Printing Museum here is well worth a visit. Natural accessory for the Kabbalists' studies, it was here that the first printing press in the Middle East was established, by the Ashkenazi brothers in 1563, just a century after the Gutenberg Bible had appeared in Mainz.

Nazareth

The town where Jesus grew up is now largely inhabited by Arab Christians—and so closing-day is Sunday—with a Jewish suburb on the northwest outskirts (total population 60,000). First mention of the town is in the New Testament, but excavations have revealed dwellings dating back to the 2nd century BC. In the modern era, Nazareth has become a major focus of reconciliation between Arab and Israeli interests. The town's construction facelift for the millennium is part of the Israeli government's investment in better relations.

Basilica of the Annunciation

Like the Dome of the Rock in Jerusalem, the modern Annunciation church's huge conical dome, 37 m (121 ft) high, dominates the urban landscape of Nazareth. It honours the spot where, according to Christian tradition, the Archangel Gabriel announced to Mary that she was to give birth to the son of god. It is the fifth church erected here, with remains of the first still visible beneath the dome, a synagogue-like structure built over Mary's grotto in the 4th century. Designed by Italian architect Giovanni Muzio, the Catholic edifice of 1955 assembles art from all over the world.

Fountain of Mary

Near the main highway from Tiberias, the fountain where Greek Orthodox Christians believe Mary experienced the Annunciation is consecrated by the church of Archangel Gabriel. Symbolically, a modern stone fountain stands just south of the church.

Ancient Synagogue

Fragments of a synagogue, honoured by Syrian Melchites as one where Jesus prayed, date in fact from the 6th century. They stand near the Melchite church beside the Arab market *(souk)*.

Mount Tabor

East of Nazareth is the pretty, dome-shaped mountain, 588 m (1,928 ft) high, scene of the Transfiguration in which the shining figure of Jesus, in the company of Moses and Elijah, revealed to his disciples Peter, James and John his divine glory —commemorated August 6. At the summit, among remains of Crusader fortifications, are a modern Franciscan church, notable for the Transfiguration mosaic in the apse, and the Greek Orthodox church of Elias (Elijah). The region's rich flora is beautifully preserved here in a nature park.

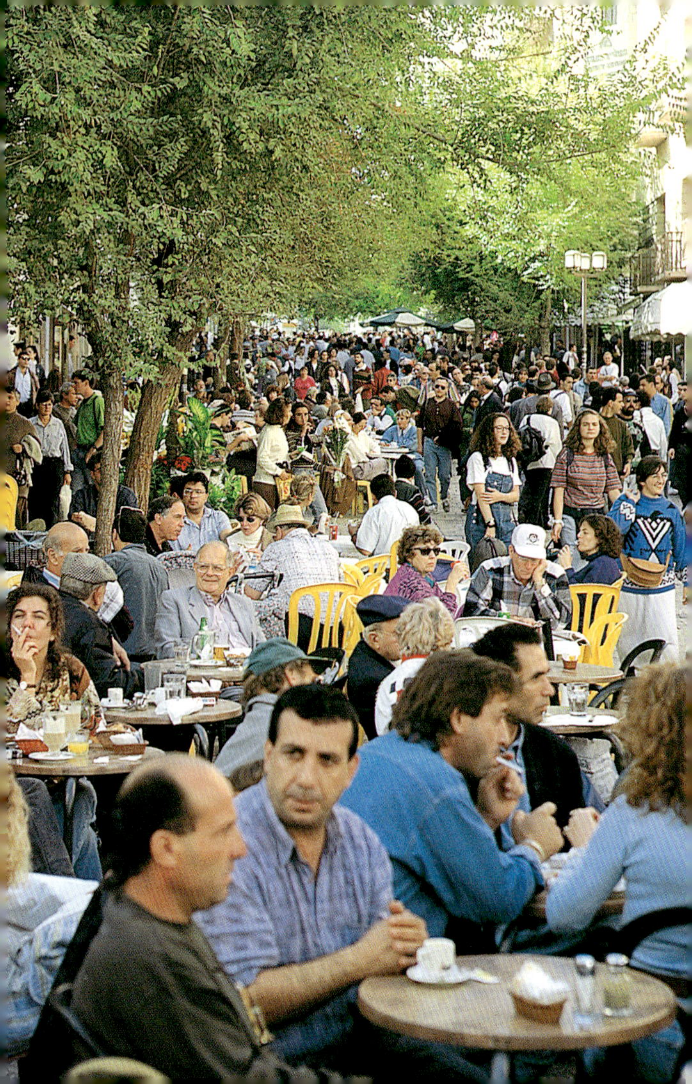

TEL AVIV AND THE MEDITERRANEAN
Tel Aviv, Jaffa, Caesarea, Haifa, Acre

Israel's Mediterranean coast is a rich mixture of city-life in Tel Aviv and Haifa, beach-bumming at seaside resorts, and historical sites such as Herod's town of Caesarea and the Crusader port of Acre.

Tel Aviv

This metropolis, counting more than a million inhabitants in the city and its suburbs, is the unabashed profane counterpart to the sacred capital of Jerusalem. What it lacks in natural and architectural beauty, it more than makes up for in the vivacity of its people. Beginning as an appendage to the port of Jaffa, it was founded in the sand dunes in 1909 as the first modern specifically Jewish city and has never looked back. It was here that David Ben Gurion proclaimed the state of Israel in 1948. Handsome old Jaffa is now its suburb.

Delivering what Liza Minnelli promises in New York, New York, Tel Aviv is really the town that doesn't sleep. What matters here is the street life, the cafés, boutiques, art galleries, theatre, concert hall and opera house.

Mediterranean life fills the streets in the buoyant city of Tel Aviv.

And on top of that, it has the beach—well-tended sand and good standards of unpolluted water—served by modern hotels, the best of them along Hayarkon Boulevard.

Dizengoff Street

In any other major city, you might start your tour at a grandiose historic monument, a temple, castle or palace. Tel Aviv has none of those. The pulse of this town is best felt on its most important thoroughfare running largely parallel to the coast four blocks in from the sea. It is named after Meir Dizengoff, first mayor of Tel Aviv. Here are the main shops, the most popular outdoor cafés, bars and restaurants. People-watching is the main sport. You will find the major art galleries on side streets like Frischmann and Gordon.

Around Habimah Square

After Dizengoff Square, the street curves east, past the huge new shopping mall called the Dizengoff Centre, to the centre of the city's cultural institutions clustered around Habimah Square. Originally founded in Moscow in 1917, the Habimah National Theatre was established here in 1935 and has two stages for its plays, performed in Hebrew but often with simultaneous translations on earphones. No translation is needed at the nearby acoustically superb concert hall of Mann Auditorium, home of the world-renowned Israel Philharmonic Orchestra. Northwest, on the corner of Leonardo da Vinci Street next to Tel Aviv Museum, is the Opera House in the city's Performing Arts Centre. Opened in 1994, this bold avant-garde structure was designed by Yaakov Rechter.

Tel Aviv Museum of Art
Set back from the broad King Saul (Shaul Hamelekh) Street, the museum has a growing collection of 19th- and 20th-century European and American art, gradually de-emphasizing the specifically Jewish character common to other art museums around the country. Its most notable European painters are Monet, Pissarro, Renoir, Picasso, Klee, Kokoschka and Edvard Munch and a superb collection of German Expressionists—Heckel, Beckmann and Schmidt-Rottluff. Major American artists represented include Mark Rothko, Jackson Pollock and Morris Louis. In addition the museum stages important international exhibitions in collaboration with major European and American museums.

Yitzhak Rabin Square
Originally Kings of Israel *(Malkhei Yisra'el)* Square, this traditional focus of mass political rallies south of City Hall was renamed after the Israeli prime minister following his assassination in November, 1995. It was during a demonstration here of 150,000 supporters of the movement for peace with the Palestinians that Rabin was shot by Yigal Amir, a right-wing Israeli

---

4 — THE FOUR BEST BEACH RESORTS Thanks to the unrivalled spectacle of its marine life in the Red Sea, **Eilat** provides the country's most elaborate water sports facilities—and the largest array of resort hotels. But **Herzliyya** and **Netanya** both offer a more relaxed, easygoing atmosphere with fine sandy beaches. And if **Caesarea** does not have exotic fish, it does have some interesting ancient ruins and a summer music festival as an alternative to baking in the sun.

TEL AVIV

extremist. A monument of raised pavement marks the assassination spot and nearby walls are papered with visitors' written homages. Appropriated by the left-wingers, the square is now the site of their electoral victory celebrations.

Sheinkin Street
Cafés, bars, nightclubs, boutiques and art galleries attract a lively young crowd to the city's most fashionable street all day and all night long. In brashly meretricious Tel Aviv, it is no accident that the best-known and longest-established meeting place here is at number 57, Café Tamar, named after a righteous maiden forced by destiny to play the harlot. The cross-street, Rothschild Boulevard, has some fine examples of 1930s architecture—note the houses at 63, 67 and 79—designed by refugees from the German Bauhaus and recently renovated.

Shalom Tower
The saving grace of this office block, 132 m (433 ft) high, is the view from the observation deck at the top. It stands at the north end of Herzl Street, Tel Aviv's first thoroughfare. When they built the tower in 1958, developers provoked huge protests by tearing down the city's first Hebrew high school, the revered Herzliya Gymnasium.

Carmel Market
Off Allenby Street is a sprawling open-air market for fruit and vegetables and for clothes, trendy and otherwise. It's a great place to come into contact with the ordinary people of Tel Aviv.

Ha'Aretz Museum
A complex of exhibition pavilions houses some splendid examples of ancient and modern artefacts dating back to Biblical times. The Glass Museum traces the history of glass-making from antiquity to modern times. The Nehustan Pavilion displays ancient copperware, tools and other implements from the pharoahs' and King Solomon's mines at Timna in the Arava valley near Eilat. Within the museum precincts is the archaeological site of Tel Qasila. It includes traces of a small harbour on the north bank of the Yarkon river that may have served to transport Lebanese cedar to Solomon's temple, and remains of a Philistine town of the 10th century BC.

Museum of the Diaspora
This magnificent museum (Beth Hatefutsoth), also located on the university campus, traces the story of the Jews' dispersal over the world after the Roman destruction of the Second Temple. The cosmopolitan tone of the experience is set by a striking

panel of photographs in the entrance hall—faces of every imaginable ethnic origin, European, African, Asian, Latin American, to show how Jews blended with societies all over the world, defying anyone to determine what is "typically Jewish". The exhibits tell the story by subject rather than chronologically—life in the family, the community, the arts, literature and politics of the nations. There are exquisite models of synagogues from ancient Turkey and medieval Germany, Toledo in Spain and Kaifeng in China, Cochin in India and Vilnius in Lithuania. A computer terminal (for a fee) helps families trace their genealogy.

Diamond Museum
Since 1936 a major industry has grown up around the decorative and industrial diamond exchange, in particular in the eastern Tel Aviv suburb of Ramat Gan. The museum on Jabotinsky Street dedicated to South African industrialist Harry Oppenheimer explains the mining and polishing of diamonds, displays some beautiful modern examples and recalls the importance of such precious stones in Biblical times.

Jaffa
Immediately south of Tel Aviv, the ancient port, among the oldest in the Mediterranean, has a past that was Canaanite, Phoenician, Philistine and Arab, but only recently Jewish. Throughout the first half of this century, it was a major focus of violent conflict between Muslim and Jew. Today, its "oriental" atmosphere contrasts with the more European-style Tel Aviv, into which it was incorporated municipally after the 1948 War of Independence. Its harbour lost its commercial importance with the development of the deep-water port at nearby Ashdod in the 1950s. The population is still largely Arab, its main shopping district more appealingly bazaar than market.

Mosque and Clocktower
Along with ornate Turkish façades on some of the seafront buildings, these distinctive landmarks underline the Ottoman presence in the town till World War I. Mahmud Pasha built the mosque in 1810, making use of ancient Roman columns from Caesarea and Ashqelon. Dating from 1906, the clocktower now has a plaque commemorating the Israeli soldiers killed in combat for the town in 1948.

Old Jaffa
The quarter out on the promontory around the old lighthouse has been attractively restored to house boutiques, craft workshops, art galleries, landscaped

JAFFA

The water is warm and the sand kept clean at Tel Aviv's beach.

gardens and seafood restaurants. The seafront promenade is especially pleasant at sunset. On the main street, notice fragments of ancient houses dating back to the Jewish Revolt against the Romans in AD 70.

Antiquities Museum
Housed in a Turkish bathhouse, the collection illustrates the history of the ancient port of Jaffa since prehistoric times. Among the sculpture, ceramics and other artefacts, a gatepost bears the seal of Egyptian pharaoh Ramses II from the 13th century BC. There is also a fine collection of Byzantine glass.

Flea Market
West of Yefet Street, sift through junk and genuine antiques—jewellery, books, furniture and other bric-a-brac. Much of it affords an intriguing insight into the possessions brought here by immigrants from Central and Eastern Europe in the 19th and early 20th centuries.

Herzliyya
What began in 1924 as an agricultural settlement named after Zionist leader Theodor Herzl has developed into a major resort city. Herzliyya's beaches attract not only foreign tourists, but streams of weekend picnickers

from Tel Aviv, just 15 km (9 miles) away. On the northern outskirts are remains of the port, fortress and city wall of Tel Arshaf, the Crusader stronghold defended by Richard Lionheart against Sultan Saladin in 1191 and razed by the Mamelukes 70 years later.

Netanya

Some 30 km (18 miles) north of Tel Aviv, the flourishing beach resort of Netanya, founded in 1928, has also prospered from its diamond industry. The centuries-old skills brought by Belgian immigrants from Antwerp to create an industrial diamond plant in World War II are now devoted to more decorative forms of jewellery.

Caesarea

The site of Roman, Byzantine and Crusader antiquities, this ancient Phoenician port city is an attractive seaside resort with hotels, restaurants, art galleries, shops and beach, with a golf course on the east side of town.

In Roman times, Caesarea was the largest city in Palestine, its name a homage to Emperor Augustus Caesar after he had presented it to King Herod. It subsequently became the seat of the Roman governor, most notably Pontius Pilate at the time that he condemned Jesus to death. It was here in AD 66 that fighting between Jewish and Greek citizens launched the Jewish Revolt that ended with the destruction of the Second Temple in Jerusalem and the final crushing of resistance at Masada.

Of Herod's fortified city, there is a spectacular Roman amphitheatre where gladiators fought wild beasts, site today of the more peaceful summer Israel Music Festival and other open-air shows. Other Roman remains include an impressive aqueduct that brought water to the town from a spring 6 km (4 miles) away, and a hippodrome not yet completely excavated on the eastern outskirts. Closer to the coast are the remains of a 6th-century Byzantine market.

But the most imposing historical buildings date from the Crusader period—from 1101 until the city's capture by the Mamelukes in 1265 and its destruction after the fall of Acre in 1291. Still standing are the city walls with gates, towers and dry moat, harbour installations and the port's fortress.

Haifa

The country's third city, population 230,000, is dismissed by many Israelis as a place where people work too hard and don't know how to enjoy themselves. But visitors without preconceptions discover, as residents have known all along, a town with a vibrant cultural life, an astonishingly varied collection of museums and, in the magnificent natural setting of Mount Carmel, elegant residential areas offsetting the relentlessly modern downtown architecture.

Haifa came into its own in the 19th century with an influx of European immigrants and the building of the Damascus–Haifa railway, and after World War I with development of the port under the British mandate. The port was a centre of Jewish immigration, both legal and clandestine, in the 30s and 40s. Yet the town apparently also has a serenity that has made it the world headquarters of the peace-loving Bahai cult.

Central Carmel

Start not downtown but in this residential district on the side of Mount Carmel. Yefe Nof (Beautiful View) Street keeps its promise with a panorama over the city, port and Bay of Haifa. In the park of Gan Ha'Em are a pretty botanical garden, small zoo and museum of prehistory.

The Port

With a permit from the information office at the entrance, tour the imposing facilities and take a cruise around the harbour. The monumental Dagon Silo, holding 100,000 tons of grain, houses a fascinating Grain Museum. It traces the history of cereal agriculture with grains of wheat 4,000 years old, ancient Egyptian murals of the pharaohs' grain-silos, Early Iron Age beer jugs and Jericho's millstones from the 8th century BC.

Bahai Temple and Gardens

The golden-domed temple is set in a beautiful Persian Garden of cypress trees. Completed only in 1953, it stands over the tomb of Ali Mohammed, founder of Babism—the forerunner of the Bahai movement, which counts some 5 million adherents around the world. The Bahai believe in a universal religion and revere equally Abraham, Moses, Jesus and Mohammed.

The Museums

The Haifa Museum on Shabbetai Levi Street groups three museums in one: ancient art, Egyptian, Canaanite, Greek and Roman; modern art, from the 18th century to the present day; and traditional musical instruments and folklore from the eastern Mediterranean.

The Clandestine Immigration Museum, 204 Allenby Road, illustrates the heroic and tragic adventures of 125,000 "illegal" Jewish immigrants smuggled into

Palestine from 1934 to 1948. You can board the tiny ship *Afalpichen* (Nevertheless) which brought 434 refugees to Haifa in 1947.

The Railway Museum in the Ottoman Haifa East Railway Station returns to the age when you could ride from Damascus, Beirut and Amman via Haifa down to the Sinai and Cairo. It displays old steam and diesel engines, freight and passenger wagons, including a splendid wood-panelled British Royal Coach dating from 1922.

Mount Carmel

The densely forested mountain, reaching 546 m (1,790 ft), whose Hebrew name means "God's Vineyard", is now a national park. Founded in the 12th century, the mountainside Stella Maris Carmelite monastery was rebuilt in the 19th century (it's accessible by cable car). The Carmelites, who take their name from the mountain, honour the prophet Elijah for his triumph over the pagan priests of Baal, and his disciple Elisha, who is said to have meditated in a nearby cave. Also on the mountain ridge is Haifa University, offering a spectacular view from the tower built by Brazilian architect Oscar Niemeyer.

The Tikotin Museum of Japanese Art, located on Mount Carmel on HaNassi Boulevard, displays its fine collection of 19th-century etchings and prints in a handsome traditional Japanese-style house.

Acre

The old port city's skyline formed by the domes, minarets and towers of mosques, Ottoman caravanserai inns and fortifications is second in charm only to that of Jerusalem itself. Acre's strategic position between Syria and Egypt has always invited invaders—Phoenicians, Assyrians, Alexander's Macedonians, Romans, Crusaders, Mamelukes, the Turks and, unsuccessfully, Napoleon Bonaparte. With attention switching to neighbouring Haifa, it can hope to preserve what is largely an 18th-century silhouette left by Bosnian-born Ahmad Pasha el-Jazzar ("the Butcher")—alongside a growing modern beach resort.

For an overall view, climb the 18th-century fortifications built on Crusader foundations.

Ahmad El-Jazzar Mosque

In classical Ottoman style with broad green dome and slender minaret, the largest of Acre's four mosques was built in 1781 on the site of the Crusaders' cathedral. It has a charming garden and ornamental fountain. Right of the mosque entrance is El-Jazzar's tomb.

Exotic and appealing, the historic skyline of the ancient port of Acre.

Crusaders' Halls
Opposite the mosque, the vaulted Gothic halls, hospital and refectory constitute an underground town for the Knights of St John. Corridors dating back to the Persians in the 7th century provided secret passage to the port.

Citadel
The fortress built by El-Jazzar over the Crusaders' quarters served in the British Mandate as a prison where Jewish underground fighters and terrorists were held.

Khan El-Umdan
The best preserved of the old town's monumental Ottoman caravanserais, or hostelries, the Inn of the Pillars is named after the Roman columns which El-Jazzar took from Caesarea. The clocktower celebrated a sultan's jubilee in 1906.

Khan El-Franj
Buried in the bustle of the Arab bazaar is the sprawling Inn of the Franks, a name attributed to all European travellers.

Fishing Harbour
The port once shared by the merchants of Pisa, Amalfi, Venice and Genoa now provides the backdrop for a number of popular seafood restaurants.

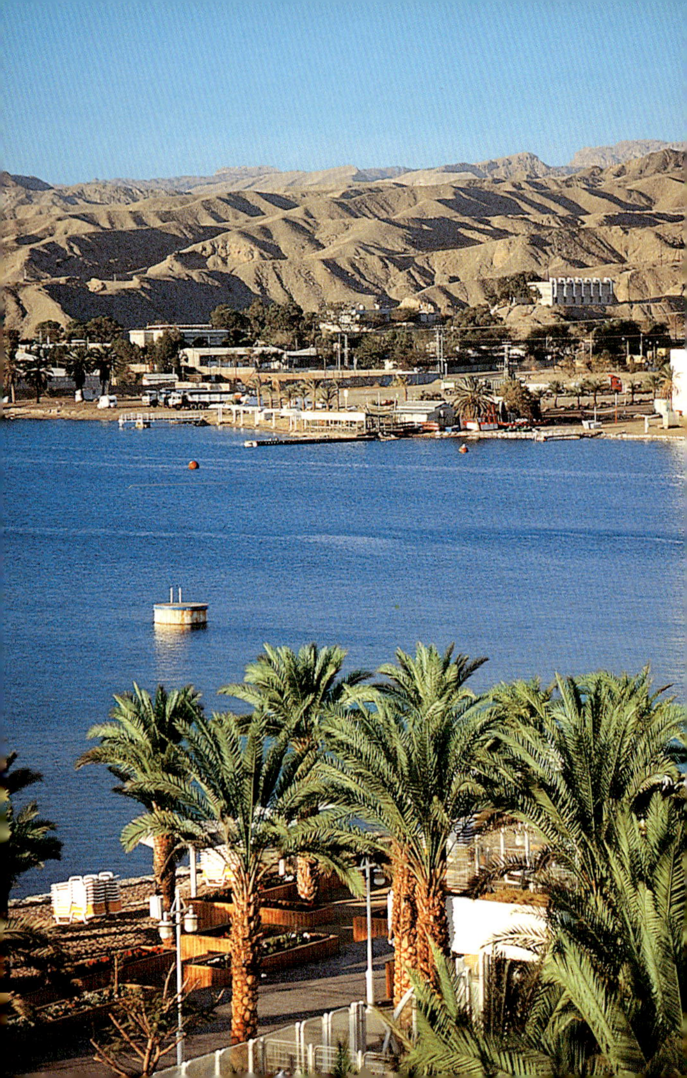

RED SEA
Eilat, Timna

The country's foremost playground has sprung up on this arm of the Red Sea known to Israelis as the Gulf of Eilat and to Jordanians as the Gulf of Aqaba.

Eilat

In 1948, it was just a couple of houses and a police station. Today, Eilat's beaches have attracted scores of hotels, restaurants and shops.

South of the harbour on Coral Beach is Coral World Underwater Observatory. A long pier leads to a chamber 5 m (16 ft) below the water, with 20 windows looking out on multicoloured exotic fish swimming free among the coral and marine plants. Apart from the huge aquarium, separate pools are provided for shark and giant tortoise.

There are three possibilities to see the fish, coral and sea-flora from a boat. The Jules Verne Explorer is a sleek little cruise boat with bar and restaurant on the upper deck and glass-windowed observation room below the waterline. The Yellow Submarine goes to depths between 25 m (82 ft) and 60 m (nearly 200 ft)—but doesn't take children under 4. Everyone is allowed aboard the more modest glass-bottomed boats.

The Nature Reserve Authority organizes guided tours to the best places for bird-watching—ideal in early spring when migratory birds make their way back from Africa to Europe.

Timna

Ancient copper mines and remains of Egyptian temples have been uncovered amid the fabulous desert landscapes of the Arava Valley 25 km (15 miles) north of Eilat. The rich veins of copper first exploited by passing nomads 5,000 years ago are once more being mined for modern industrial purposes. The pharaohs began mining here around 1400 BC, an industry continued by King Solomon 500 years later.

Solomon's Pillars

These dramatic natural pillars 50 m (160 ft) high, hewn from the sandstone cliffs by the wind, form part of Timna Park's presentation of the ancient mines. Opposite the fancifully named pillars are remains of an Egyptian mining camp and the vestiges of a temple dedicated to the earth-goddess Hathor. Up on the rock face you can see a carving of Ramses III. An artificial lake has been created to offer a little cool relief for picnickers.

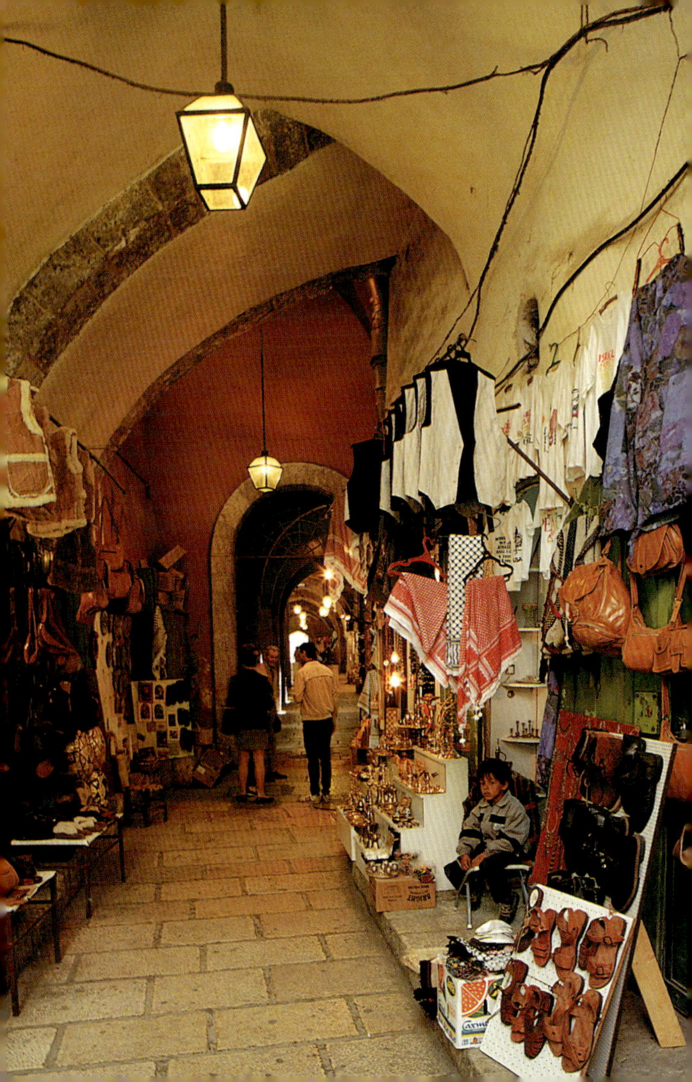

Shopping

The cosmopolitan character of the Israeli people, with origins from every continent, is reflected in what you may find in the shops. The fashion boutiques in Tel Aviv—and increasingly Jerusalem, too—display original variations on sophisticated French or Italian designer clothes. But you will also find traditional folk costumes and jewellery made by Yemenite or Ethiopian Jews that might have graced any lady-in-waiting on the Queen of Sheba's visit to King Solomon. Not forgetting the wealth of craft goods available in the Arab markets of Jerusalem and Bethlehem.

Where?

Bazaars, both Arab and Jewish, in Jerusalem's Old City, are a pleasure to explore, as much for fascinating local colour as for what you might find there. Many of the modern city's shops are located in the mainly pedestrian zone bounded by Jaffa Road, Ben Yehuda and King George V Street. You can't stop progress—the new Jerusalem Mall *(Canyon Yerushalayim)* on the southwest outskirts makes up in convenience for what it lacks in holy-city charm. In exuberant contrast is the Makhane Yehuda street market.

In Tel Aviv, besides the parallel shopping streets of Dizengoff and Ben Yehuda, boutiques and galleries abound in the restored section of Old Jaffa. Jaffa also has a fine Flea Market west of Yefet Street.

Outside Jerusalem, the best Arab craftwork is to be found on and around Bethlehem's Manger Square and in the old bazaar *(souk)* of Acre.

What?

These days, international trade means that everything is available everywhere, but you can still find things, profane or religious, that immediately say *Israel*.

Antiques

The more fortunate immigrants, particularly from Germany and Eastern Europe, brought with them some fine old pieces, anything from furniture to silver hair-

SHOPPING

brushes, gold watches and fountain pens. Israeli proverb: "A young boy's Barmitzvah present is an old man's antique." To export antiquities from before 1700, you will need to obtain written authorization from the Department of Antiquities in the Rockefeller Museum (Jerusalem). Another Israeli proverb: "If it's worth taking, they won't let you. If they let you, it's not worth taking."

Books, Maps and Prints

Fine editions of Bibles and prayer books, reproductions of medieval maps of Jerusalem and the Holy Land, and of 19th-century prints by British artist David Robert are easy to find.

Clothes

Silks are well designed and leather finely crafted. Most distinctive of all, however, are the Yemenite and Bedouin embroidered shawls, long skirts and dresses in simple cotton.

Computer Software

Word-processing kits are available in Hebrew with English or French. The wonders of CD-Rom memory-storage put the Talmud and Bible in Hebrew on compact discs. You can also get Hebrew-English/French pocket electronic translators, containing 30,000 words.

Craftware

Religious souvenirs in olive wood and mother-of-pearl have been crafted in Bethlehem practically since the location of Jesus' birthplace was identified in the 4th century. Popular items for Christian pilgrims are traditional figures for the Christmas crib: Holy Family, the three Kings and the Good Shepherds. Jewish religious items include brass or silver *menorah* candelabras, ornate *mezuzzah* signs for the doorpost and embroidered silk bags for prayer shawls.

Jewellery

For the best selection in high-price jewellery, go where it's made and traded—the Diamond Exchange in the Tel Aviv suburb of Ramat Gan and up the coast at Netanya.

There is also a National Diamond Centre outlet in Jerusalem. In Jerusalem's Old City, you will find reasonably priced gold and silver, and even better bargains in traditional Yemenite and Bedouin earrings, necklaces, bracelets and rings. Watches come with the digits in Hebrew or Arabic.

Music

Buy classical or Israeli and Arab folk music on cassette or compact disc, very often at a good discount if you pay cash.

Dining Out

It's not yet terrific, but it's getting better. Cuisine in Israel's pioneering days was, like the formalities of bourgeois manners, not a priority. Now with growing peace and prosperity, people are taking time out for the good things of life. They travel abroad and discover international tastes. With a population from the four corners of the earth, they have every kind of national cuisine, kosher dietary laws notwithstanding.

So What Is Kosher?

Without going into all the minute details of "keeping kosher"—which only a tiny minority of Jews manage to observe in their entirety—the basic requirements are: no pork, ham or anything else from the pig, and no shellfish; and, from the Biblical law that forbids the cooking of the kid-goat in the milk of its mother, no mixing in the same meal of meat and dairy products—milk, butter, cheese, etc. Now that is not so terrible. Pork is not the best thing to eat in a hot country, anyway, and Israeli chefs offer smoked turkey as a very good substitute for ham. Just save the ice-cream desserts for your fish dinners. In any case, not all restaurants are kosher, particularly outside Jerusalem. Like everything else in Israel, kosher food is political, with many secular Jews as ostentatious in their refusal to eat it as the Orthodox are about observing its laws.

To Start With...

A few Eastern European restaurants offer traditional chicken soup with *kneidlech* (dumplings) or *kreplach* (a kind of Yiddish won-ton); cabbage or beetroot soup; or the perennial *gefilte fish*, minced fish-balls, classically carp cooked in fish broth and served cold with *khrein,* a hot horseradish sauce sweetened with beetroot. Middle Eastern and North African restaurants offer Turkish-style *tahina* (purée of sesame seed), *hoummous* (chickpea purée) or chopped aubergine (eggplant) salad, or *tabouleh* cracked-wheat, mint and parsley.

Fish or Meat?

The great fish delicacy of Israel bears the joyfully Christian name of St Peter's fish, the delicious, large lake-perch grilled whole at the Sea of Galilee. Otherwise, the best fresh fish is to be found at Jaffa, mainly in non-kosher Arab restaurants. Trout, mullet or sea bass are likely to be freshly caught rather than frozen only in the high-priced restaurants.

Lamb or mutton comes in traditional European style, chops or roast, or in the Turkish manner, *shwarma,* sliced off the spit, shashliks or kebabs. Kurdish-Iraqi restaurants near Jerusalem's Makhane Yehuda market make excellent stuffed veal-breasts *(pishta mazo)* and savoury meatball *(kubbeh)* dishes. Ethiopian cuisine tends to be hot and curried beef, lamb or cabbage and yellow beans. Hungarians offer goulash, roast goose and stuffed cabbage. Memories of cold winds blowing off the steppe or the Polish plain justify the persistence of the robust fatty meat stew served with beans and potatoes as a Sabbath "delicacy" known as *choolent.*

If you want an honest-to-goodness steak, look out for Argentinian grills, reared on the Galilee pampas and kosher.

Desserts

The cheesecake is better in New York or London, the ice cream so-so, but the sweet blintzes (pancakes), apple strudel and pies can be great. Otherwise go for Turkish-style *baklava* pastry or a slice of *halva,* made from sesame seeds, honey and nuts. Best of all is the fresh fruit: plums, peaches, apricots, pomegranates, figs—ah, the figs, ask Solomon.

Drinks

The wines are getting better all the time. The Rothschilds at last got round to bringing in their know-how and vines from Bordeaux. Of course, they taste a little different here, but the reds are more than honourable, best of all the Gamla and Yarden currently grown up on the Golan Heights. Already, the wine-growers have a game-plan for a strategic withdrawal to Galilee, if necessary.

Home-brewed beers are light, American-style—Gold Star and Maccabee. If you are partial to syrupy sweet liqueurs, *Sabra* is a mixture of orange and chocolate. Safest and very, very good are the fresh fruit juices.

Coffee for all tastes: apart from instant, you'll find good Italian espresso, but beware of the cappuccino's whipped cream; Turkish is found particularly in Arab neighbourhoods; and you'll also come across a rough-and-ready Israeli version called *bots,* which literally means "mud", boiling water poured onto the ground coffee, stirred with the sugar which, if left to settle and sipped carefully, can be quite delicious.

Sports

The abundance of sporting pleasures in Israel guarantees that your visit does not have to be one long gruelling grind of sightseeing.

Water Sports

The beaches at Tel Aviv, Netanya, Herzliyya, Caesarea and, of course, Eilat are first class, but don't forget Tiberias and En Gev on the Sea of Galilee. After your first dip in the Dead Sea at Ein Gedi or En Boqeq, you will probably prefer the swimming pool.

Eilat's water sports facilities on the Red Sea are as good as any you will find in Europe, with the added attraction of marine fauna, coral and flora providing a spectacle that no Mediterranean resort can match—with visibility to depths of 40 m (130 ft). You can rent equipment and get expert training for snorkelling and scuba-diving. Depending on your taste and budget, amenities at these resorts are also available for water-skiing, windsurfing, parasailing, kayak and yachting.

Tennis and Golf

Besides the bigger hotels' hard courts, often floodlit, you will find public tennis courts in Jerusalem, Tel Aviv, Haifa and Tiberias. Caesarea boasts, rightly, an 18-hole golf course right by the remains of the Crusader and Roman city.

Hiking

…or if that sounds too strenuous, rambling, has been a Jewish sport since the Exodus from Egypt. It is still well organized—by the Society for the Protection of Nature, headquartered in Jerusalem, with an excellent shop for maps and books. The ultimate hike through the Promised Land has been mapped out from Mount Hermon in the north all the way south to Eilat, and it doesn't take 40 years.

Spectator Sports

Just two count for anything here —basketball and football (soccer), in that order. The Tel Aviv and Haifa basketball teams are up there with the top Europeans. Football at club level is played with the same philosophy as the army: never retreat. As a result—unlike the army—Israeli teams generally have terrible defense. Somehow at the national level they do better.

The Hard Facts

To plan your trip, here are some of the practical details you should know about Israel:

Airports
With the exception of charters to Eilat, international flights come into Ben-Gurion Airport, 20 km (12 miles) from Tel Aviv and 45 km (28 miles) from Jerusalem. The terminal provides banking, car-hire and tourist information office services, in addition to duty-free shop, restaurant and snack bar facilities.

Climate
Israel has a remarkably varied climate. Summers are hot and humid on the Mediterranean coast from Tel Aviv to Haifa, hot and dry in Jerusalem, milder in Galilee but stifling on the Dead Sea and in Eilat. The best time to go is spring or autumn. Up in the Judaean Hills, Jerusalem is blessedly mellow, always a few degrees cooler than the coast. Eilat is a delight in autumn and winter, when Tel Aviv is pleasant but Jerusalem cold and wet. On occasion, the holy city has had to draw on the snow-clearing expertise of the new Russian immigrants. Galilee enjoys its own mild climate, even in winter.

Communications
Israel has installed a highly modern telecommunication system for fax and phone. Call worldwide with telecards from pay phones, much cheaper than the hotel's surcharge service. In a country boasting the world's highest rate of mobile phone ownership, you can rent one locally just for the period of your stay.

Crime
Israel is a predominantly honest place. Pickpockets—very often a fellow tourist—may be a problem at the beach, in crowded street markets or in buses. Without being paranoid, don't tempt them with an open handbag or a wallet in the hip pocket. Put valuables in the hotel safe.

Driving
If renting a car, be sure to have a valid national licence or International Driving Permit. Rental age limit is usually over 21. Credit card payment exempts you from VAT. Check on the exact extent of varying insurance coverage;

personal, fire, collision, theft, etc. Drive on the right, overtake on the left. Israeli drivers are fast, impatient but basically competent. The new network of highways is first class.

Electric current
220-volt 50-cycle A.C., but with a three-pin plug different from the British. Hotels can usually provide adaptors.

Emergencies
Most problems can be handled at your hotel desk. Telephone number for police: **100**. Like most other countries, Britain keeps its consulate in Tel Aviv, but consular help is there only for critical situations, lost passports or worse, not for lost cash or plane tickets. (The USA has consulates in both East and West Jerusalem.)

Essentials
You won't need much formal wear. Pack a sunhat and add a sweater for cool evenings. Good walking shoes are vital, especially for the desert, and easy-to-kick-off sandals or moccasins for the mosques in Jerusalem and Arab towns. Don't forget insect repellent and a pocket torch (flashlight).

Formalities
A valid passport is all that most of you will need. Have the Israeli visa stamped on a separate form if you visit Arab countries that refuse entry for passports bearing an Israeli stamp. No special health certificates are required for European or North American citizens.

Customs controls are minimal at point of entry, with an official import allowance, duty-free, of 250 cigarettes, 2 litres of wine and 1 litre of spirits. No limit on amounts of foreign currency.

Health
The big health hazard in Israel is the sun. Watch out for sunstroke, heat exhaustion and dehydration. Stick to the shade, wear a hat, use a good sunscreen, drink litres of water, it's as simple as that. Unless otherwise stated, it's perfectly safe to drink the tap water. For emergencies, make sure your health insurance covers holiday illnesses. Doctors, dentists and hospital staff are very competent, most speaking good English. If you expect to need prescription medicines, take your own as you may not find the exact equivalent on the spot.

Holidays and festivals
Israel's public holidays follow the Hebrew calendar.
September/October:
Rosh Hashana New Year
Yom Kippur Day of Atonement

THE HARD FACTS

Sukkoth   Tabernacles
Simchat Torah Feast of the Law
Late November/December
(shops stay open):
Chanukah   Feast
                    of the Lights
March/April:
Pesach   Passover
April/May:
Independence Day
May/June:
Liberation of Jerusalem
Shavuoth   Feast of Weeks

The chief Muslim holidays are Mohammed's birthday and the fasting month of Ramadan. Easter and Christmas are particularly big in Jerusalem, Bethlehem and Nazareth.

Languages
English is the most common "second" language after Hebrew. In the city centres, street signs are most often written in Hebrew and English—and occasionally also in Arabic.

Media
Besides the European and American periodicals, Israel has two English-language newspapers: the daily *Jerusalem Post* and bi-monthly *Jerusalem Report.*

Major hotels have satellite dishes for BBC and CNN television. BBC and Voice of America radio are all easily accessible on short wave. *Kol Israel* state radio and TV have daily news bulletins in English.

Money
The Israeli unit of currency is the shekel, officially NIS (New Israeli Shekel), divided into 100 agorot. Coins: 5, 10 and 50 agorot, 1, 5 and 10 NIS. Banknotes: 10, 20, 50, 100 and 200 NIS. Shops and restaurants welcome credit cards, as well as Eurocheques and traveller's cheques. U.S. dollars are still a favourite secondary currency. Payment of hotel bills and car rentals in any foreign currency, credit card and traveller's cheques exempts you from V.A.T.

Opening hours
The following times are given as a general guide, some of them subject to variations. *Banks* open 8 a.m. till 12.30 p.m. Sunday to Thursday, till noon on Friday, opening again for an extra hour or so at 4 p.m. on Sunday, Tuesday and Thursday. *Shops* are open till lunchtime Sunday to Friday, and again from 4 to 7 p.m. Sunday to Thursday. Muslim shops close on Friday, Christian shops on Sunday. *Main Post Offices* open 8 a.m. to 6 p.m. Sunday to Thursday, closing Friday at 1 or 2 p.m.

Photography
Be discreet if you photograph devout Jews, Muslims or Christians. It is strictly taboo in the

THE HARD FACTS

Orthodox neighbourhoods on the Sabbath.

Public Transport

Buses and trains do not run on the Jewish Sabbath from Friday sunset to Saturday sunset. Arab-operated services, notably from East Jerusalem and Nazareth, run every day. Bus services of the Egged and Dan companies are generally clean, efficient, and most often air-conditioned, running from 5 a.m. to 11.30 p.m. The train between Jerusalem and Tel Aviv is more folklore than transportation, but the service between Tel Aviv, Haifa and Nahariya is pretty good. For travel between cities, *sherut* shared taxis, 8-passenger limousines, are best value for money, more comfortable and only 20 per cent more expensive than the bus. Hotels and tourist office will advise on pick-up places.

Time and Date

Israel's time zone is GMT +2, i.e. putting its clocks 2 hours ahead of London, 7 hours ahead of New York, 11 hours ahead of Los Angeles. The clocks are put forward an hour in March for daylight saving and back again for Rosh Hashana, usually in September.

The Israeli calendar observes both the Jewish and ordinary months. the Jewish year is calculated according to a biblically ascertained Creation date of 3761 BC (so that the Christian year 2000 is 5761 in the Jewish calendar. In Israeli publications, BC and AD often become BCE (Before the Common Era) and CE (Common Era).

Tipping

Add a little extra to the service charges that are included, by law, in hotel and restaurant bills.

Toilets

In general, public toilets are good and hygienic. They are usually signposted in Hebrew, English and Arabic.

VAT Refund

A sales tax refund can be obtained for purchases of more than $50 worth of goods from stores registered with the Ministry of Tourism (not valid for electrical appliances, photographic equipment and tobacco). For reimbursement (in U.S. dollars, minus commission), show goods and V.A.T. form to a Bank Leumi official at Ben-Gurion airport.

Websites

Some useful Israeli websites include the Tourist Ministry's www.infotour.co.il; the Foreign Ministry's www.israel.org; and a search engine for Jewish and Israeli subjects www.maven.co.il

INDEX

Abu Gosh 29
Acre 50–51
Avdat 35
Beersheba 34–35
Belvoir 38
Bet She'an 8, 39
Bethlehem 31
Caesarea 48
Capernaum 38
Dead Sea 32–34
Eilat 44, 53
Ein Gedi 33
Ein Kerem 29
En Boqeq 34
En Gev 37
Galilee 36–41
Haifa 48–50
Hebron 32
Herzliyya 44
Jaffa 46–47
Jericho 33
Jerusalem 19–29
　American Colony
　　Hotel 27
　Ben Yehuda
　　Street 25–26

Bible Lands
　Museum 28
Bukhara 26–27
Church of Holy
　Sepulchre 23–24
Church
　of St Anne 23
Damascus Gate 23
Dome of the Rock 22
El-Aqsa Mosque 23
Garden Tomb 27
Israel Museum 28
Jaffa Gate 20
Jewish Quarter 21
King David
　Street 26
Knesset 28–29
Makhane
　Yehuda 26
Mea She'arim 26–27
Mount of Olives
　24–25
Mount Scopus 28
Mount Zion 25
Rockefeller
　Museum 27

Russian
　Compound 26
Souk 23
Supreme Court 28–29
Temple Tunnel
　21–22
Tower of David 20
Valley of Kidron 25
Via Dolorosa 22
Western Wall 21
Yad Vashem 29
Judaean Wilderness
　31–32
Masada 33
Nazareth 41
Negev 34–35
Netanya 44
Qumran 32
Safed 39–41
Sea of Galilee 37–39
Sede Boqer 35
Tabgha 38
Tel Aviv 43–46
Tiberias 36–37
Timna 53
Zefat see Safed

General editor: Barbara Ender
Layout: Luc Malherbe
Photos: front cover José Nicolas/Hémisphères; back cover, pp. 10, 52 F. Brot;
pp. 6, 18, 35 E. Mandelmann; pp. 12, 24 H. Satz; p. 42 R. Magnes;
pp. 30, 54 Pawel Wysocki/Hémisphères; p. 47 Sandu Mendrea; p. 51 B. Joliat
Maps: Elsner & Schichor; JPM Publications

Copyright © 1999, 1995 by JPM Publications S.A.
12, avenue William-Fraisse, 1006 Lausanne, Switzerland
E-mail: information@jpmguides.com
Web site: http://www.jpmguides.com/

All rights reserved. No part of this book may be reproduced or transmitted in any form or by any means, electronic or mechanical, including photocopying, recording or by any information storage and retrieval system without permission in writing from the publisher.
Every care has been taken to verify the information in the guide, but the publisher cannot accept responsibility for any errors that may have occurred. If you spot an inaccuracy or a serious omission, please let us know.
Printed in Switzerland—Gessler/Sion (CTF)　　　　　　　　　　　Edition 1999–2000

JERUSALEM OLD CITY

ISRAEL
N
0
10 km
JORDAN
Jordan
Dead Sea
Mediterranean
SHOMERON
TEL AVIV-JAFFA (YAFO)
JERUSALEM (Yerushalayim)
Naplouse/Nablus (Shekhem)
Jéricho
Georgskloster
Nabi Musa
Qalya
Qumran
Mar Saba
Bethlehem (Betlehem)
Beit Jālā
Allenby Bridge
Karāma
Damiya
Hamra
Mekhora
Beit Fūrik
Rujeib
Aqraba
Majdal Bani Fadil
Qabalan
810 m
803 m
857 m
Rafidiya
Funduq
Kefar-Tappuah
Salfit
Arura
Sinjil
Tomer
Kafr Malik
Kokhar Ha Shahar
Aujā et Tahtā
Yabrūd
Ofra
Deir Dibwan
El Bira
Kafr'Aqab
Jaba'
Bir Zeit
Umm Safā
Rāmallah
Bir-Nabala
Anātā
Biddū
Qirat-Anavim
Moza
Ora Aminadav
Bar-Giyyora
Matta
Zanoah
Beit Sira
Mevo Horon
Abu Gosh
Eshta'ol
Zor'a
Bet-Shemesh
Sedot Mikha
Ziyyon
Har'el
Beqoa
Tal-Shahar
Tirosh
Kefar Menahém
Revadim
Gedera
Arugot
Quiryat Mal'akhi
Hazor Ashdot
Be'er Toriyya
Shetulim
Kefar Ha No'ar Nizzanim
Ashdod
Gan Yavne
Bene-Darom
Kefar-Aviv
Shedema
Yavne
Kefar Ha Nagid
Giv'at Brenner
Benaya
Quirat-Eqron
Yesodot
Gezer
Na'an
Azaiya
Kefar-Shemu'el
Gimzo
Ramla
Rehovot
Nes-Ziyyona
Rishon-Le Ziyyon
Lod
Hadid
Budrus
Ni'lin
Kharbata
Beitillū
Qibya
Shuqba
Abūd
Kafr ed Dik
Alé Zahav
Masha
Sanniriya
Kafr Thult
'Azzun
Kafr Jammal
Nirit
Kafr Qasim
Rosh Ha'Ayim
Nahshomin
Petah-Tiqwa
Yehud
Bene'Atarot
Tirat-Yehuda
Kefar-Truman
Ben Gurion
Zetan
Bet-Dagan
Holon
Bat Yam
Or-Yehuda
Savyon
Qiryat-Ono
Iv Atayim
Ramat-Gan
Bene-Berao
Ha Yarqon
Ramat-Ha Sharon
Hod Sharon
Herzliyya
Kefa Shemaryahu
Shefayim
Ra'ananna
Bazera
Tira
Qalqiliya
Kefar-Sava
2
4
40
44
1
3
38
55
57
60
90